CORKING
the
BOTTLE

A DAY-BY-DAY GUIDE TO A SOBER LIFE

Terri
All the best in sobriety.

Dan Hicks

D0839669

Dan Hicks

ISBN 979-8-88851-119-0 (Paperback)
ISBN 979-8-88851-120-6 (Digital)

Covenant Books
11661 Hwy 707
Murrells Inlet, SC 29576
www.covenantbooks.com

WHY THIS BOOK?

Hi. I'm Dan. I'm an alcoholic.

Ashamed of myself? Not anymore. *Regretful?* Still am, but I have my regrets under control. *Self-loathing?* Never have been, really. *Forgiving of myself?* Yes, but I had to learn how. *Forgiving of others?* Again, it's an ongoing learning experience. *A drunk?* Not anymore. *Alone?* I found my place. *Religious?* No. *Spiritual?* That's a big yes! I believe that God is like a classroom teacher, giving us pop quizzes and hard tests. Someday I will take my final exam. But first, I want to share something with people battling addiction, searching for faith, seeking real joy in their lives. I am such a person and have made strides toward bringing order and meaning to my life. It's an ongoing process. Our God-given tests keep coming, and each exam that we pass makes us a better person, if we let it.

Some people fail God's tests, even when he gives them the answer sheet or allows them to copy from someone else's paper. Yes, for a long time, I kept failing too. I wondered what was wrong with me. In my case, I kept drinking. And then I drank some more. I hated the repercussions, but I drank again anyway. I didn't know why. My life, once orderly and neat, became chaotic. It wasn't my fault, I told myself. It never was my fault.

Sometime in my fifties, drinking changed from an occasional relaxing evening to all-day binges. I don't know when it happened exactly. Maybe it was just before my first drunk-driving arrest or maybe the second. Anyway, I'm sure I was an alcoholic before my two car accidents that I don't remember. What I do remember is how God slowly began to help me turn my life around. I question anyone who claims to have found sobriety before first discovering

1

God along the journey. There's no chicken and egg. God comes first before sobriety.

Alcohol addiction was the biggest test of life. I kept digging myself deeper and deeper until I broke the shovel and climbed out of the pit. God was the proctor and the answer, but I failed to see it for several years. Some take longer to get well, some find a cure quicker. The time it takes is less important than the time we have left in our lives to be sober, to find God, to find joy, to find ourselves. I'm glad to be an alcoholic. That's how I found God and let him take over my life. I quit doing my will and turned that will over to him. You can too. There's nothing so special about me that you can't duplicate.

Once we are on the road to recovery and know where we want to go, we discover we are selfish unless we GPS our route for others to follow. There isn't a right or wrong way to get to where we want to go, but there are plenty of highways out there. Whatever works for you is God's miracle. Find it. Maybe my way will work for you, maybe it won't. It's the destination, not the journey, that counts. As my sponsor, Danny, once said, "No matter how far down the road you go, you're still the same distance away from the ditch."

My birthday—the date of my sobriety—is May 1, 2018. The summer that followed, I felt God leading me (more like a firm shove) to begin a blog, to share what I was discovering with others. One of his greatest gifts to me has been the ability to write and, most of the time, make sense with my words. That's how I became a newspaper reporter and corporate magazine editor. Writing about my ongoing recovery seemed like a way to use this verbal gift God gave me. "You are good at something for a reason. God designed you this way, on purpose. It isn't fake or a fluke or small. These are the mind and heart and hands and voice you've been given, so use them" (*For the Love: Fighting for Grace in a World of Impossible Standards* by Jen Hatmaker).

I think God wanted more people to read my God-inspired posts. That's where the idea for this book came from. I am going back through my blog posts, editing them as I see fit for this medium. I will head each message with the numbered day of my sobriety. I start with May 13, the thirteenth day of my sobriety. As you read my posts for each day, I encourage you to look for my growth as a sober child of God. See if you can identify with my anecdotes and my proselytizing. Come with me on my journey of recovery through my higher power I call God. I write because I am inspired by AA's Step 12: *Having had a spiritual awakening as the result of these Steps, we tried to carry this message to alcoholics, and to practice these principles in all our affairs.*

Sober day 13
The troubled tale of a struggling drunk

I am going to summarize here my life's successes, which later seemed to crumble and lead me to alcohol. It's not to brag but to explain how good things were for me and how losing them dragged me into a downward spiral. I am an unusual drunk. I never drank as a kid. As a young and middle-aged adult, I drank socially; yeah, sometimes too much, but I wasn't thinking about my next drink afterward. Drinking wasn't a problem. I had a wonderful childhood raised by teetotalling parents who loved each other and taught me and my three kid sisters to love. I grew up in Beaver Falls, Pennsylvania, about thirty-five miles north of Pittsburgh. Dad was a high school math teacher; mom was a stay-at-home mother. We didn't have much, but we had all we needed. I was a straight-A student. School came easy. I decided in high school to become a journalist and took advantage of writing opportunities in and outside of school. I won awards. I landed a part-time sports-writing job at our local newspaper, *The Beaver County Times.* This led to a full-paid scholarship to Point Park College (now University) in downtown Pittsburgh based on writing ability, so college was totally free.

I graduated a year early because of college level tests I passed, got a job as news bureau manager in my mother's hometown of Grove City, Pennsylvania, where I still had lots of relatives, and jumped into my newspaper job the day after my last final exam. I married my childhood sweetheart at the same time I started a public relations job, where my salary doubled overnight from my journalism job. A feature story I wrote for our company newspaper I edited led me into marathon running, and I ran dozens of races through the next decades. Back in college, I volunteered one summer on the Nez Perce Indian reservation in Idaho and fell in love with the Northwest.

One day, I wrote to a PR director in Boise, got a job interview the same week, and was offered a job on the spot. That's when we moved to Boise, two years into our marriage, which I might add was going wonderfully. That job was awful, so after six months, I wrote to another corporation in Boise that happened to be looking for a writer. I got that job and more money.

See what I mean? My life was so good and so full of triumphs. We had two splendid daughters (who are still splendid as adults) and enjoyed a close family life, often camping and hiking in the mountains. We were active in our Presbyterian church and, for a while, hosted a weekly Bible study in our home. I could go on, but I think that's enough to show I had a Midas touch. If something didn't work out for me, something better came along. That's the way life's supposed to be, I thought. We wanted to move back closer to home in Pennsylvania in 1989, and sure enough, I landed my best job ever in Louisville, now driving distance instead of flying distance from family and "home" in western Pennsylvania. I worked at that company for sixteen years.

Then the wheels came off and life spun out of control. I was laid off on the day, almost, of my fiftieth birthday. Several would-be employers turned me down for jobs, some after interviews, and some without responding to my applications. Even fast-food joints weren't interested in me. I got a part-time job with a crisis communications firm, but it wasn't the same as the community relations work I had come to enjoy so much. I lived off my 401(k) and pension and my wife's income from working the zoo gift shop. Cripes, we used to be making six figures together! Not anymore.

My marriage felt strained, and intimacy became a fond memory. My older daughter resented the time I was spending as a volunteer with disadvantaged kids and jealously accused me of getting too friendly with little girls. She quit speaking to me. Kids in the youth program I had created grew up, and some of them chose to wallow in the ditches I had tried to lead them out of. Some had families and good jobs, but all I could see were the addicts and criminals I had watched grow up.

I had arthroscopic knee surgery, which pretty much ended my running career. I started gaining weight. My beard turned white. I denied my depression for a long time before I got help from my doctor. But the mood-altering pills didn't work well enough. Alcohol worked better. My drinking increased. My thoughts were of poor, pitiful me. There seemed to be no solution. The good life was over. My wife was ready to leave me. Good! That would give me another reason to drink. I got two DUIs. I was fined heavily, lost my license, and placed on in-home incarceration. I was hospitalized twice with alcohol poisoning. I ignored the hospital social worker's talk about AA. At my wife's urging (i.e., nagging), I finally entered a local rehab outpatient program, then a twenty-eight-day inpatient program, then more outpatient, then group counseling, and so on and so on. I have done that and lots more to end my addiction, which I will write about in future posts.

All worked, but only for a little while. I started into AA. Sometimes I went to therapy and AA meetings a little bit drunk. I got kicked out of two group programs for showing up inebriated. I didn't care much. I am two whole weeks sober as I write this (insert Bronx cheer here). I have found God and made spirituality part of my life and my path to wellness. So there is still hope for me. I feel strongly God led me to start this blog, which now I am turning into a book. It is intended to help other suffering relapsers like me and ultimately lead *me* to a sober life (insert real cheer here). Writing this is therapeutic. May God give you strength to get well and do his will.

Sober day 14
"Right now" is a happy place to be

One of my character defects that led me to become addicted to alcohol was my longing for the past. As I outlined in yesterday's introductory post, I had a great life that eventually soured. I lost most of what I lived for or so it seemed to me. I learned in group therapy at Better Alternatives Counseling that I needed to live in the moment. I couldn't return to the past, and I couldn't plan my way into someday getting back all I had "lost." Live in the moment! Here is a video that explains why living in the moment is a healthy way of being. It lasts four minutes and sixteen seconds. I rounded up a few quotes you may find inspirational:

"What day is it?"
"It's today," squeaked Piglet.
"My favorite day," said Pooh. (A. A. Milne)

You must live in the present, launch yourself on every wave, find your eternity in each moment. Fools stand on their island of opportunities and look toward another land. There is no other land; there is no other life but this. (Henry David Thoreau)

You can't go back to how things were. How you thought they were. All you really have is… now. (Jay Asher, *Thirteen Reasons Why*)

Dance. Smile. Giggle. Marvel. Trust. Hope. Love. Wish. Believe. Most of all, enjoy every moment of the journey, and appreciate where you are at this moment instead of always focusing on how far you have to go. (Mandy Hale, *The Single Woman: Life, Love, and a Dash of Sass*)

> Learn from yesterday, live for today, look to tomorrow, rest this afternoon. (Charles M. Schulz, *Charlie Brown's Little Book of Wisdom*)

Sober day 15
Symptoms of alcoholism

I often hear newbies wonder if they have an alcohol problem. For me, the best evidence is if I can make my planned last drink of the day really my last drink, and do I find myself thinking of alcohol and looking forward to my next close encounter of the "fifth" kind?

I found some other symptoms of alcoholism when I looked over this website:

> For those who are on the fence, there's another important question to ask: Has alcohol negatively impacted your health? Though health and wellness is a broad category to consider, the most specific thing to look at is physical health. Do you ever wake up with "the shakes?" Have you noticed more intense bouts of anxiety or depression? Do you feel foggy or forgetful? Have you sustained any physical injuries due to drinking?
>
> While the above are only short-term issues, the CDC reports that problems like these can intensify if left unchecked. More serious health issues caused by heavy drinking may include high blood pressure, heart disease, stroke, cancer, dementia, digestive issues, alcoholism, coma, and even death.
>
> Still, health is not limited only to physical issues but also to other aspects of your life, like relationships, for example. Have you noticed any recurring issues with your romantic partners or significant other? If you're a parent, has there

been any tension between you and your children? Do you have a balanced and fulfilling social life? Do you have a healthy sex life or are you prone to risky and impulsive behaviors?

While the answers to the above questions may not be directly related to your alcohol consumption, studies have shown that excessive drinking can negatively affect a variety of our social behaviors as well as our actual health. Perhaps most important to consider in all the above is that all of these problems are avoidable. Without having to resort to labels like "alcoholic" or "addict," *the first step to recovery is the desire to find a better way of life. For those who feel their life has become unmanageable with their current drinking habits, all that remains is to ask for help.* (emphasis added)

Asking for help was the hard part for me. But I felt better when I finally reached out.

Sober day 16
Wisdom at AA

I heard a couple good one-liners at my AA home group meeting today.

Jim: 'What keeps us from being happy? We don't let go of the things that make us sad." I am guilty as charged. Sometimes.
Mark: "If I drink, my problems will have puppies. I'm not much, but I'm all I think about."

Sober day 18
A reason for it all

Everything happens for a reason—even alcoholism. I'm still searching for my reason, but I know it's out there somewhere. I must stop relapsing, learn patience, and trust God. Maybe my reason for drinking is to remake my character. Maybe my reason is to write this blog. Maybe one or more of you who read this site will be inspired in some way. I dunno, but there must be a reason for my Buick to be steered into a ditch. I like what the *Big Book* (the AA bible) says on page 457:

> *So as I have worked the program, I have grown emotionally and intellectually. I not only have peace with God, I have the peace of God through an active God consciousness. I not only have recovered from alcoholism, I have become whole in person—body, spirit, and soul.*

It is a paradox, but alcoholism is helping me become a better person.

Sober day 19
Give me that old-time spirituality

I grew up as part of a family active in church. There, people told me what to believe. And I did believe. But later, in my adult life, I became disillusioned with formal religion as it was taught to me. In my community relations job, I became painfully aware of basic needs being unmet. It seemed churches didn't know or else didn't care about the people living all around them who were struggling to be healthy families. I no longer felt religious, but I still believed in God. What's up with that? It wasn't until I got into AA that I learned religion and spirituality are different. I can be spiritual: love God, pray, seek to do God's will, and *don't judge others' spirituality*. I believe there is one God, but how I perceive him is up to me. We choose our own higher power. I had never seen spirituality from this perspective. Where you find your higher power doesn't matter. Just find it!

One of my favorite books is *Awakening in Time* by Jacquelyn Small. She writes, "When we honor the higher power's principles of love—of truth, goodness, and beauty—we are using our energy as a creative positive force, and we feel serene. When we violate its laws of love and wisdom, which are in fact our nature, we feel isolated, heavy, uninspired, and out of sorts... In order to connect with our higher power, we simply need to be still and listen. Our intuition already knows the sound of its voice."

Sober day 22
Is alcoholism a disease?

I have been told and have read, since I was knee-high to a bourbon barrel, that alcoholism is a disease. That's still my opinion, and I'm sticking to it. But a book I am currently reading, *Scripts People Live* by Claude Steiner, contains a different view (page 233). I will save you the wordy reasoning, but he writes that "real" diseases require microorganism changes to some organ. No such bodily alterations cause mental illnesses and no drugs cure them, leaving afflictions like addictions as "undiseases." He goes on to claim, "At present no drug has proven effective to cure depression, madness, or drug abuse...since these tragic scripts are not the result of chemical or micro-organismic changes in the body but the result of the scripted interactions between people... Thus, alcoholism is not an illness."

Not so fast, Claude. AA's *Big Book* disagrees. So do *Staying Sober* authors Terrence T. Gorski and Merlene Miller (pages 39–40):

> Addiction is a physical disease. It is properly classified with cancer, heart disease, and diabetes as a chronic illness that produces long-term physical, psychological, and social damage. Like victims of these other diseases, alcoholics have physical conditions that have caused them to be susceptible to developing this disease.

Drugs *are* available, Claude. I take pills for depression and recently started on Antabuse, which will make me very sick if I drink alcohol. These aren't cures, but diseases like diabetes have no cure either, just medicine to ward off the symptoms.

Sober day 23
What the Big Book says

Here is a follow-up to yesterday's question of whether alcoholism counts as a disease. It so happens an AA *Big Book* study meeting I attended yesterday offered this analysis. You will find it in the personal stories section in the back of the book on page 205. A woman in the 1930s era of AA had this to say: "I was a sick person. I was suffering from an actual disease that had a name and symptoms like diabetes or cancer or TB—and a disease was respectable, not a moral stigma!" I like that—"not a moral stigma."

Disease or not, having alcoholism doesn't make me wicked or immoral. Categorize it however you like. I'm not a bad person because of it. I'm a person in need of help. In my case, I got that help, and now I look to help others in whatever ways I can. Just call me Dr. Dan.

Sober day 24
Baseball, summer nights, and—what is missing?

This is a big day for me. I am going to Cincinnati to watch my Pirates play the Reds. I grew up near Pittsburgh, and although I moved away a long time ago, I remain loyal to its sports teams. I have seen lots of games in Cincinnati, mostly when Pittsburgh is in town. The beer is too expensive to tempt me (it was like $8 a shot last year), but I miss a cold beer on a hot day while watching baseball. Those were relaxing and stress-relieving days. I got addicted to the devil's distilled drinks, not beer. I got too full on beer. Hard liquor gave me the feeling I was seeking without all those bloated trips to the bathroom. It is unfortunate I have to give up beer with baseball. I just hope I am wise enough to understand that it's better to give up beer (even on $1 beer night) than sacrifice my liver. This evening, I will concentrate on baseball with a clear mind. Beat 'em, Bucs!

Sober day 25
Talking and listening to God

I shared with my AA home group members today that I started this blog. I explained I felt I had heard God speak to me and tell me writing these posts would help me and help others. God's suggestion to write came as a bump in the night—except it was daytime, and I was sitting in the sunlight on the back porch. Nevertheless, trust me: It went bump. I pray, but more important, I have conversations with God throughout the day. Sometimes it's to express gratitude for something, sometimes it's to ask for health and safety of loved ones. Heck, sometimes it's even to ask for health and safety of idiots when they drive by me like maniacs. By speaking to God, I can hear his will for me. Sometimes. I ask, daily, for him to let me know his will, then help me carry it out. That's what led me to start this blog.

When I was a wee little lad, I had an invisible playmate named Loodie. It just occurred to me that maybe Loodie was really God. Hmm. It's worth me considering this new idea. She was so real to me that, one day, my mom got mad and took Loodie from the table and threw her outside. I cried until Mom went to the backyard and carried Loodie back in.

Try it. Talk to God as a friend. Maybe he will be your own Loodie.

Sober day 26
Becoming the exorcist

I don't believe in exorcising spirits, but I sure do believe in exercising spirits. No priest or holy water is required for the latter. A good pair of shoes and maybe some Gatorade, and you are all set to exercise. Your spirit soon will be in good spirits. Workouts are essential to the health of all, but an alcoholic needs workouts as much as he or she needs an AA sponsor to feel in shape. After I finish writing this post, I will brave the Kentucky heat to take a brisk walk through my neighborhood. It's a far cry from my prime when I ran marathons and often twenty-mile-plus training runs. Bad knees, old age, and alcohol have all taken a toll on my physical well-being.

Nevertheless, I can't allow myself to collect cobwebs in my easy chair, so I walk or use my elliptical machine in the basement or cut grass and do other yard work. If going to the gym, riding a bike, or swimming are more your athletic cup of tea, go for it. Just do something to raise your heart rate for at least thirty minutes, four days or more per week. I do extra most days because I have some extra fat calories to burn up. Alcohol added calories and pounds to my physique. Exercise is as good for our brains as it us for our brawn. When we exercise, our brains get a dose of the same chemicals that once made drinking feel good. Dopamine is a pleasure chemical that is released during and after physical exertion, even light exertion. If you think a drink is going to make you feel better, instead of giving in to evil temptations, go for a walk. After a half hour or so of walking and thinking, then see if you still need that drink. One day at a time, one workout at a time.

Sober day 27
Who made me judge and jury? Not God!

I am Facebook friends with many people I graduated high school with forty-five years ago (almost to the exact day!). Some of them I hung around with in school and out. But many of them I barely knew. Some I can't remember at all. But each one brings to the keyboard some kind of wisdom. They are parents and grandparents. Some have strong political views. Some have good jobs. Some, like me, are retired. All seem to have contributed to society and other former classmates in some way. When I was in high school, I rarely and barely spoke to some of these "friends." If they weren't getting all As and Bs in the classroom, as I was, I dismissed them as potential friends. I guess I figured they would end up working on a steel mill floor, waiting on customers at Kaufman's, or dumping trash cans into a truck. We had nothing in common.

Yes, I was *that* arrogant! I still had a touch of better-than-youism when I started with AA. At least there I knew we all shared at least one thing in common. But as I read Facebook posts from high school "rejects" and got to know AA people from all backgrounds and all economic levels, I finally learned an important lesson, albeit a little late. Arrogance was one of my biggest character defects. Sobriety meant fixing my defects. It meant understanding that God created all of us equal and has important tasks for us to do with the talents he gave us. I hope I wasn't judged as narrow-mindedly as I judged others. Now that I have rediscovered the God of my understanding and know that he loves us all the same, I have been able to shed my arrogance. Some of it, at least. It's a work in progress. By doing so, I find great learnings from *all* people I come in contact with—face-to-face and Facebook to Facebook.

Sober day 28
Who opened the trapdoor on my stage?

All the world's a stage, according to Shakespeare. Oscar Wilde said it more accurately with "the world is a stage, but the play is badly cast." I have a leading role, I'm afraid. And as an alcoholic, I find the world is actually four stages. I will go through the stages and my experience in each.

Stage 1: Occasional alcohol abuse and binge drinking—I drank once in a while. No problem, eh? I drank too much on weekends when I was home alone and my wife worked. If I had no place to go, I was fine drinking and sleeping my way through dull days.

Stage 2: Increased drinking as a coping mechanism—After I was laid off from my job of sixteen years, I filled my time tutoring, working for a consulting firm, and drinking in between. This was my depressed period. I denied to myself and those close to me that I was depressed or that I was self-medicating with alcohol. I knew alcohol was a depressant and was contributing to my depression. But without a drink (or three or five) now and then, my inner conversations dragged me down. I earned my vodka, I thought.

Stage 3: The consequences of problem drinking start to show—I was fired from tutoring because I was suspected of showing up drunk. They were so stupid. No one could tell I was drinking, I told myself. I was facilitator for an industrial/community committee. I called in "sick" at the last minute a few times, lost the minutes to one month, and got a letter that my performance had slipped and I was being replaced. That cost me a nice check every month. They hired the wife of the plant manager who had sent me the pink slip. Ha! He just wanted his wife to make all that money. There was really nothing wrong with *me*.

Stage 4: Noticeable physical and psychological changes—I was still in denial, even though my longer stretches of sobriety led people to tell me I was looking good. I tended to slack off of my exercising when I was drinking or when wishing I were. I get a physical every year from my primary care physician, and all my body parts were still functioning normally, I was told each time. But I could feel myself losing my balance and lacking coordination, even during my dry spells. No matter what stage of alcoholism someone is currently experiencing, there is still hope to get through their alcohol addiction. Medically supervised detox followed by an inpatient treatment program can increase the likelihood of successful recovery and help people regain control.

Sober day 30
Some defects we can't return to the store

Discovering character defects means coming face-to-face with the bad "us." Until I take action to admit my defects to God, myself, and another human being (Step 5), and then relegate oopses solely to the rearview mirror, I am stuck with staring down the ugly me. How do I refrain from beating myself up for what suddenly seem to be obvious flaws? A book I have read twice is *Awakening in Time* by Jacquelyn Small.

She gets a bit heady for me with chakras and their respective glands and colors (whatever all that means), but I highlighted many parts of the book to refer to later. One such passage helps me accept myself, defects and all:

> From the Higher Self's perspective, I do not judge my weaknesses and vulnerabilities as "bad;" I simply note them for what they are—with compassion. I see that I'm not perfect. But at the same time, I know that I am also a mature person. I'm doing the best I can and am willing to grow and learn. I quit feeling shame and allow myself to see and honor my childish or threatened self, which just naturally has some character flaws.

My prayer today: God, may I use my character defects (like drinking) to do your will.

Sober day 32
This chip isn't on my shoulder

At an AA meeting today, I received my red chip in recognition of my thirty days of sobriety! If you've never been here where I am in my program, you might be tempted to pooh-pooh this small step. But this is my first red chip. I have several silver chips, given for twenty-four hours or a desire to stop drinking. I passed that road mark again and again, only to relapse and start over. This time, I made it all the way to thirty days. Making it to sixty and ninety and beyond seems like a high, steep mountain to climb. But remember, it's like trying to eat an elephant. How do you eat an elephant? One bite at a time.

Sober day 34
One step at a time or maybe all six or maybe none

I carry in my wallet, at all times, my six defenses to fend off relapse temptations. Yours will be different than mine. You need to come up with what will help you. After I share my defenses, I will then share a secret with you.

1. Do something else. Take a walk, go to a meeting, etc.
2. Read some self-help books including, but not limited to, the *Big Book.*
3. Eat something spicy or sweet.
4. Call my sponsor or someone else who can help—including my very own little sister.
5. Call my wife.
6. Start over with #1.

Now for the secret I promised. Every time I relapsed, I ignored my six defenses. I decided I wanted to drink, and, doggonit, I didn't want anything to stop me. After all, I can quit anytime, I will just drink a little at a time, I will only drink at night, I will only drink on weekends, blah, blah, blah. Write down your own defenses, *and then follow them!* Don't do as I do. I mean as I *did.*

Sober day 35
It's only skin deep

I had an appointment with my dermatologist today. It occurred to me that she is a lot like God. They both remove defects if I let them.

Sober day 37
Feeling good requires 729 pages

As I understand Freud, he spent a lot of time discussing child-hood, relationships with parents, and the Oedipus complex. My psy-chiatrist turned me on to a book he thought might be helpful.

Boy, he was right! I am now reading it for a second time. It is full of good stuff to help me get to the real root of my hang-ups. It's about cognitive therapy, which says my relationship with my father isn't all that significant. The book is *The Feeling Good Handbook* by Dr. David D. Burns. It would be difficult to delve into many specifics because the theory is hard to explain in a few short blog posts. (Burns' book is two inches and 729 pages including the index). Maybe a website on cognitive theory will pique your interest. One to try is:

That site describes cognitive theory this way:

> Cognitive-behavioral therapy is a rela-tively short-term, focused psychotherapy for a wide range of psychological problems including depression, anxiety, anger, marital conflict, lone-liness, panic, fears, eating abuse, *alcohol abuse*, and dependence and personality problems. The focus of therapy is on how you are thinking, behaving, and communicating today rather than on your early childhood experiences. The thera-pist assists the patient in identifying specific dis-tortions (using cognitive assessment) and biases

in thinking and provides guidance on how to change this thinking.

In other words, it's up to me to alter my thinking so I can diagnose and heal myself. More later.

Sober day 38
Get off the gas and shift gears

Liza's dad is kicking her younger brother out of their house because he won't or can't stop abusing. Judy is moving, which will leave her abusing son with no place to go. Dealing with consequences stinks, but we made choices that led us to these dead ends, and unless we can turn the car around, it's a long walk back to the highway.

Mark pointed out at AA that we didn't choose to start attending AA meetings because we thought it would be a fun place to hang out. It's the largest organization no one ever wanted to join. Instead, we had to accept consequences of the choices we made. We learn at meetings that it's never too late to turn our lives around. Many of us have a lot of mechanical work to do first, and that can take a lot of time and effort. AA is just one of the tools we can use to get our engines running like new again. What's in *your* toolbox?

Sober day 39
Remembering days of wine and whine

I just watched *Days of Wine and Roses* starring Jack Lemmon and Lee Remick (1962). It's a story of an alcoholic couple who loved each other and loved their daughter. It took Jack Lemmon (Joe) several tries to stay sober. Lee Remick (Kirsten) had a tougher time. In the end, Joe had to tell Kirsten they couldn't be together anymore until she wanted and received help. Joe offers to reconcile with Kirsten, but only if she quits drinking. "You remember how it really was? You and me and booze—a threesome. You and I were a couple of drunks on the sea of booze, and the boat sank. I got hold of something that kept me from going under, and I'm not going to let go of it. Not for you. Not for anyone. If you want to grab on, grab on. But there's just room for you and me—no threesome."

The TV narrator said Jack Lemmon and Director Blake Edwards both drank heavily together during the filming, ironically. She claimed they both got help later.

Sober day 40
Well, I never!

I never worry about being driven to drink. I just worry about being driven home.

I never drink anything stronger than gin before breakfast.

I never drink water because of the disgusting things that fish do in it. (W. C. Fields, 1880–1946)

Laugh at your problems; everybody else does. (Seneca the Younger)

Sometimes my character defects are up and dressed before I am. (Someone at AA)

Sober day 41
Step lively

Mark at AA, today, quoted someone he had heard speak of his higher power like this: "I can't. He can. I think I'll let him." Huh? Look at the first three AA steps.

Step 1: "*We admitted we were powerless over alcohol—that our lives had become unmanageable.*" I can't.

Step 2: "*Came to believe a Power greater than ourselves could restore us to sanity.*" He can!

Step 3: "*Made a decision to turn our will and our lives over to the care of God as we understood Him.*" I think I'll let him!

Sober day 42
Dr. Jekyll? Better Hyde!

A 2015 study published by *Addiction Research and Theory* identified four kinds of drunks:

(1) Hemmingway. These drunks show minimal signs of intoxication despite their heavy drinking. I used to think or wish that were me.
(2) Mary Poppins. They are agreeable when sober and still agreeable when drunk.
(3) The Nutty Professor. These people are extremely introverted when sober and become the life of the party when blasted.
(4) Dr. Jekyll/Mr. Hyde. They have the personality of Dr. Jekyll when sober but turn into violent monsters when drunk.

The study cited is at:

An *MEL Magazine* article by Jennifer Sanchez sheds some light on Mr. Hyde. She refers to David Friedman of the Wake Forest University School of Medicine, who has been conducting drug abuse research for nearly forty years. "You probably won't be surprised to hear this, but some people are just angrier or more hostile than others," Friedman explains. "And it's the angry folks who get angriest when they're drunk."

However, as you might expect, it's not that cut-and-dried. There are actually three factors that change people from Jekyll into Hyde.

They are a mixture of *personality, neuroscience,* and *social context. Personality* means those who regularly suppress their anger let it out when under the influence. And, certainly, those who are aggressive, to begin with, compound this character defect when they drink.

Neuroscience refers to the way alcohol affects almost all the chemical systems in the brain. A few drinks can short-circuit communication between different parts of the brain, including the prefrontal cortex, the epicenter for decision-making and judgment. Someone prone to anger when sober might be even less likely to refrain from it when drinking.

The third factor of drinking violence is *social context.* "Alcohol makes it harder for people to interpret facial expressions, which is a complex thing to do," Friedman points out. "It's particularly difficult to distinguish threatening from submissive when under the influence. So, here you are, you're a little bit angry to begin with because that's your nature, your self-control is weakened (by alcohol), and you look at the guy at the other end of the bar, and what may be a neutral or nonthreatening face suddenly becomes threatening. Then you act out."

There is one sure way to keep yourself from being an angry or violent drunk: *Don't drink!*

Sober day 45
Higher power comes lovingly in all shapes and sizes

I had a Sunday school teacher when I was in high school who believed the Bible was the infallible Word of God, no questions asked. That kind of blind belief was met by teenage doubts and questioning. One Sunday, she left the room to let us discuss "firing" her. We did. Our new teacher allowed us to openly discuss Bible stories, what they meant, and if they were literally true. She let us listen to *Jesus Christ Superstar.* I never lost my faith in a higher power, but I never found him/her, for example, as one who flooded the entire earth while sparing Noah and his ark full or who handed Moses a list of rules etched on stone tablets.

Today's AA Daily Reflection says:

> I couldn't accept the concept of a Higher
> Power because I believed God was cruel and unlov-
> ing. In desperation I chose a table, a tree, then my
> AA group, as my higher power. Time passed, my
> life improved, and I began to wonder about this
> Higher Power. Gradually, with patience, humility
> and a lot of questions, I came to believe in God.
> Now my relationship with my Higher Power gives
> me the strength to live a happy, sober life.

At my home group meeting today, Jim said he stumbled down that same road. "The coffee pot used to be my higher power, but it ran empty. Then the doorknob was my higher power, but it turned on me." We must come to believe in some form of a higher power if we ever are going to get and remain sober. If you don't see a burning bush, try a doorknob. The truth, eventually, will come and set you free.

Sober day 46
The past has passed, so let it go

Longing to return to my past was a major factor that led me to abuse the bottle. A resource I find helpful, loaned to me by Leslie of Better Alternatives Counseling in Louisville, is *The Power of Now* by Eckhart Tolle. She loaned me a boxed variety of fifty inspirational cards. Here are a few samples:

"How to stop creating time? Realize deeply the present moment is all you ever have. Make the Now the primary focus of your life."

"Acceptance of what is immediately frees you from mind identification and thus reconnects you with Being. Resistance is the mind."

"Enlightenment means choosing to dwell in the state of presence rather than in time. It means saying yes to what is."

"Observe how the mind labels an unpleasant moment and how this labeling process, this conscious sitting in judgment, creates pain and unhappiness."

Sober day 47
Smooth sailing from this pair o' docks

Today's paradox: I regret the way I used to live, but I love that life that has been left behind in ruins. I wouldn't know people I know, I wouldn't know the self I know now, and I wouldn't be able to help those still struggling with alcohol addiction. This passage from *Staying Sober* by Terence T. Gorski and Merlene Miller reminds me of the me I used to be. Sound familiar?

> Mood swings are common as the person uses the drug to feel better but is unable to maintain the good feelings. As life becomes more and more drug centered, there is less and less control over behavior. Activities that interfere with drinking or using are given up. Getting ready to use, using, and recovering from using become the life activities of addicted people. They do things while drinking they would not do sober. While sober, they structure their lives to protect their using. They break promises, forget commitments, lie—all to be able to use. Isolation is common... Drug seeking behavior becomes a lifestyle.

Far better to center lifestyle around trusting God, cleaning house, and helping others.

Sober day 48
Happy Dad's Day

Today is Father's Day. I don't get into made-up holidays like this one, but I will pause to give thanks to my father. He shaped me, led me, and left me too soon. Dad died of a heart attack in 1979, just a month after his forty-ninth birthday. I was married and out on my own by that time, but I lost my best friend that day. I had called him that morning because I had an extra ticket to the Pirates game in Pittsburgh, but he was at church, working on something. I went without him.

Dad emphasized three attributes in life, and he followed them all. He didn't want me ever to smoke, swear, or drink. As time has passed, I have learned that obeying two out of three wasn't good enough. I now pass up alcohol and am trying to make it a hat trick for my father. It wasn't easy, but he never told me it would be.

Sober day 49
Passionate about drinking?

My dad was a funny man. I mean the good kind of funny— quick wit, loved puns, and carried a quiverful of jokes. Most were moaners. Here's one. I hope it comes off in writing as well—no, better—as it does orally:

A woman was in a bar for hours and clearly had too much to drink. A policeman happened to be there and insisted he drive her home. They got into his police cruiser, where he soon asked, "Okay, where do you live?"

The inebriated woman put her hand on the officer's arm and slurred, "Yer passionate."

"Please, ma'am. Just tell me where you live."

She put her hand on his hand on the steering wheel. "Yer passionate."

"Please, lady. I'm a happily married man. Now tell me where you live!"

"I did. Yer passhin' it."

Sober day 50
Everyone is special (Mister Rogers)

I used to be the community relations manager for a chemical plant. Part of my job was meeting people, talking about our operations, and listening to concerns. "I can smell your company, so I know that's why I feel bad all the time," some believed. Too often, the monologue went like this: "I have breast cancer. My husband died of lung cancer. Our son has asthma. I know of at least six people on my street who have had cancer. I'm ready to sue y'all. Son, go out to the car and bring me my cigarettes."

No one can say if our emissions were the cause of cancer or asthma or the common cold. One out of four people will get cancer no matter where they spend their lives. We worked on reducing emissions and odors, constantly, but we were dealing with coal boilers and odiferous chemicals that evaporate easily. It's like the gasoline smell when you fill up your car. It's like baking bread and inhaling all that wonderful odor. Some molecules escape and get sucked up our nostrils.

Staying Sober, by Terence Gorski and Merlene Miller, calls addictive disease bio-psycho-social. They write:

> Like victims of…these other diseases (cancer, asthma, diabetes, allergies), alcoholics have physical conditions that have caused them to be susceptible to developing the disease… Some people are born with a body more susceptible to addiction than other people.

I have heard speakers at AA meetings say they are certain they became alcoholics as soon as they took their first drink. For me, I started drinking at eighteen and drank in moderation until I was in my fifties. Then I no longer could stop after the first drink. And the next day, I needed another. So, go ahead, expose children to second-hand smoke, move next door to a chemical plant, soak your liver in alcohol. Maybe you will get sick. Maybe you will die young, and maybe there will be no effect. You are the one who chooses whether to play Russian roulette. Want to pull the trigger?

Sober day 51
The foot bone's connected to the ankle bone, I think

When it comes to hands, I'm not very handy. When it comes to following written instructions, A+B=3 for me. I set the directions to anything aside and try to figure out how all the pieces go together and in what order. I *always* have to tear it apart and start over. If the directions are sketches with minimal words, I find nothing in real life looks like the illustrations. And when the instructions are comprised of both words *and* pictures, I might as well go straight to the Japanese translation because that will do me just as much good.

Thank the god of my choice that life comes with clear instructions. They are called the 12 Steps. They're not just for alcoholics and addicts, but for anyone looking for a better life. Unfortunately, few people follow them. See:

For me, those steps once were a stairway to nowhere. It wasn't until I spent twenty-eight days at The Brook in Louisville, where we worked Steps 1–7, that I came to understand how those 12 could help me. I still don't have the nerve to do Step 9. I hope that doesn't make me a hypocrite or a quitter. I keep Steps 10–12—the ongoing forever steps—in front of me. That's how I can continually better myself and help others. So that you don't have to go to the website referred to above, here are Steps 9 to 12 for your convenience:

9. *Made direct amends to such people wherever possible, except when to do so would injure them or others.*

10. *Continued to take personal inventory and when we were wrong promptly admitted it.*

11. *Sought through prayer and meditation to improve our conscious contact with God as we understood Him, praying only for knowledge of His will for us and the power to carry that out.*

12. *Having had a spiritual awakening as the result of these Steps, we tried to carry this message to alcoholics, and to practice these principles in all our affairs.*

The 12 Steps aren't easy, for sure. But work your way through them in order, and you will be rewarded. It's not as bad as following some other directions and trying to find tab A to put into slot B.

Sober day 52
I'll get you, my pretty! And your little dog too!

It must have been the first time I watched *The Wizard of Oz*. I was in first grade or younger; my sister was a year and a half younger than I. When the witch came on the screen—although all we had was a black-and-white TV—she was still scary enough that I can remember how that fear felt. My sister hid behind the couch and cried. I still feel fear, but it's a different kind. That movie was fight-or-flight fear. I felt threatened by danger, even though the danger was irrational. My fears, these days, remain irrational fears like will I make someone mad? Will people not like me? Will my kids give up on their alcoholic father? According to Dr. David D. Burns in *The Feeling Good Handbook*:

"When you avoid frightening situations, you simply make your problem worse… Facing your fears will help you conquer them. You learn the catastrophe you fear will not really happen." Doing so is uncomfortable at first. Like speaking up at an AA meeting. No one gets mad, and people get to know me and actually like me. As faced fears diminish, we often find fear is replaced by exhilaration and pride.

Pay no attention to the man you fear behind the curtain. Pull the curtain all the way back and expose him for what he really is. And be assured that drinking never conquered fear permanently. "We have nothing to fear but fear itself," except for the Wicked Witch of the West!

Sober day 53
The Big Book is a bestseller

Quite by accident, I stumbled upon (a sober stumble, not one of my inebriated trips) a website that dishes out some interesting perspectives on the success of AA and the so-called *Big Book* that steers that organization, and it says:

> Today, AA is serving more than 2 million recovering alcoholics in more than 180 countries. Moreover, the 12 Step program that Bill W. laid out in the Big Book has helped millions of people with a host of other addictions. "These include Narcotics Anonymous, the more specific Marijuana Anonymous, Gamblers Anonymous, Workaholics Anonymous, and Sexaholics Anonymous," reports the BBC. Clutterers Anonymous deals with those with hoarding problems. Underearners Anonymous offers support for those suffering an inability to provide for one's needs. Support for loved ones of those going through addiction is on offer at Families Anonymous (more common around here is Al-Anon).
>
> In 2011, the Big Book was named one of the most influential books written in English by *Time*. In 2012, the Library of Congress named it one of the 88 books that shaped America. More than 35 million copies of the Big Book have been sold since 1939.

Sober day 54
Kneeling hurts far less than marathon running

I used to be a marathon runner. If you could see me, you would be laughing now. My knees creak, my belly sags, and I moan going downstairs. But it's true. In the springtime of my life, I ran twenty-nine marathons, a fifty-miler, and lots of races from five to eighteen miles, and thousands of training miles to remain fit. But after knee surgery and a prolonged bout of laziness, I am reduced to walk/jog about thirty to forty minutes a day. Once healthy and fit, I now find I am tired after mowing the lawn or vacuuming the house or flicking through channels with the remote.

Lesson: To retain one's physical fitness requires regular effort, through rain or snow or sleet or (recently) heat. Likewise, I once let go of my spiritual fitness. I stopped praying, stopped caring, and started drinking to excess. I was a lost cause. Thankfully, God didn't let me stay lost among the tall weeds in the rough. He lifted me onto the fairway, drove me to the green, and led me to the hole.

Lesson: To retain one's spiritual fitness requires regular effort, through anger or selfishness or envy. I am pleased to say I am back on track with my spiritual fitness and back on *the* track with my physical fitness.

Sober day 55
How to build sand castles without a beach

I was about to lose my job in 2004. My friend, confidant, and sister-in-law, Karen (all rolled into one), must have sensed a high-pressure weather system and impending rainstorm. She told me I should go sit on a beach until I find the real Dan again. Of course, I didn't take her advice. *"We thought we could find an easier, softer way. But we could not"* (*Big Book*, page 58). At that point, I was still frantically digging my hole deeper and deeper and deeper but hadn't hit bottom yet.

Today, I find the old Dan is no more. It turns out the hole he was digging was his own grave. But from all the depression, DUIs, fender benders, and blackouts arose a new Dan. I seriously never have felt like this in my entire life. I feel no stress. I am empowered. I am in control of my life. I discovered true joy. I made a decision to turn my will and my life over to *"the care of God as we understood him."*

Further, I made a moral inventory of myself and *"was entirely ready to have God remove all these defects of character"* and then humbly asked him to do so (Steps 3, 4, 6, and 7). I still wish I had gone and lost myself on some beach. But the new me was born from the debris I was hanging onto. I substituted AA meeting rooms and therapy for that beach. And now, I'm a whole new me. I am grateful to God and to Karen.

Sober day 56
Can you define "God?"

Someone at my home group meeting today said something I really liked. We were discussing the AA Daily Reflection, which said, in part, "The 12 Steps have helped to change my life in many ways, but none is more effective than the acquisition of a Higher Power." A man at the meeting said he used to worship a lower power—alcohol—and he was his own higher power. I can relate. Another shared that he can't define God but said you can feel him inside you if you are open. From the AA *Big Book*, page 60: *"God could and would if he were sought."*

Sober day 57
In the driver's seat—Part 1

Take a minute. What guides your life? The correct answer here is God. But all of us—some of the time, all of the time, or part of the time—are driven by painful, bad stuff. If you are reading this, maybe you are being driven by alcohol or other drugs. *The Purpose Driven Life* gives us five common "circumstances, values, and emotions" that take the wheel as we drop God off at a bus stop in Kalamazoo or somewhere. This is a wonderful book written by Rick Warren that gives me lots of "oh yeah" moments. Here are his top drivers. For the next five days, I will write a little about each. They are:

1. Many people are driven by guilt.
2. Many people are driven by resentment and anger.
3. Many people are driven by fear.
4. Many people are driven by materialism.
5. Many people are driven by the need for approval.

I will dissect each like a frog in a high school biology class.

Sober day 58
In the driver's seat—Part 2: guilt

I asked, yesterday, what drives your life? Rick Warren, in *The Purpose Driven Life,* suggests five drivers that often distract us from what really *should* be driving our lives:

Guilt—In my case, regret of my past, at times, has me driving into a ditch. I have to work at forgetting the pain I caused myself and the people who love me and steer between the lines. "Guilt-driven people are manipulated by memories. They allow their past to control their future. They often unconsciously punish themselves by sabotaging their own success."

I did things in my drinking days that really hurt. They cost me lots of money and lost me the trust of loved ones. I can't change any of that junk, so I work at living today, in the now. "We are products of our past, but we don't have to be prisoners of it. God's purpose is not limited by your past."

Sober day 59
In the driver's seat—Part 3: resentment and anger

Some of us would rather get even than get healthy. We bottle up our hurts and never get over them. Instead, we react poorly. "Some resentment-driven people *'clam up'* and internalize their anger, while others *'blow up'* and explode it onto others. Both responses are unhealthy and unhelpful." The past is gone. The person we think wronged us probably has forgotten about whatever it is that keeps you resentful. No one who hurt you in the past can continue to hurt you unless you allow them. "For your own sake, learn from it and then let it go."

Sober day 60
In the driver's seat—Part 4: fear

I asked what drives your life. Rick Warren, in *The Purpose Driven Life*, suggests five drivers that often distract us from what really *should* be driving our lives. Yesterday, it was anger and resentment. Today, *fear*—"Fears may be a result of a traumatic experience, unrealistic expectations, growing up in a high-control home, or even genetic predisposition."

In my case, as an adolescent, the fear that drove me was a fear of rejection. That's what kept me from asking girls to go out with me. I was afraid my life would be ruined if a girl told me "No." So I stood back and watched my friends be brave. While they were in the game, I was on the sidelines, feeling alone. Whatever fear may drive you, it causes you to miss out on opportunities. You decide not to take risks and hope everything will turn out all right. "Fear is a self-imposed prison that will keep you from becoming what God intends for you to be." I was in Sing Sing yet couldn't carry a tune.

Sober day 61
In the driver's seat—Part 5: materialism

Some are led by a desire to acquire. So what? If I have many possessions, won't that make me happy, feel important, and more secure? Nope. "Possessions only provide temporary happiness. Because these things do not change, we eventually become bored with them and then want newer, bigger, better versions." Next, possessions don't make us more important. "Self-worth and net-worth are not the same." And more secure? Material things can be lost by theft, flood, fire, or sometimes divorce (you know if I'm talking to *you*). "Real security can only be found in that which can never be taken from you—your relationship with God." God is the way to sobriety!

Sober day 62
In the driver's seat—Part 6: need for approval

Here goes the last part of this series. *The need for approval*—this was really me. I guess it still is. I was overwhelmed with a need to please my parents. I kept my hair a certain way, wore certain clothes, listened to certain music, and, for the most part, followed the rules of the house. Same in school. I remember being a tattletale. That didn't win approval from my classmates, but I believed I was grabbing positive attention from my teachers. It all seems silly now.

"Unfortunately, those who follow the crowd usually get lost in it. I don't know all the keys to success, but one key to failure is to try to please everyone. Being controlled by the opinions of others is a guaranteed way to miss God's purposes for your life."

How about you? Are any of these five drivers, highlighted here, steering your life in the wrong direction? Recognizing them is the first step to controlling them. Time for some self-reflection, don't you think?

Sober day 63
I've got that joy, joy, joy, joy down in my heart

I'm not happy all the time. No one is. When I get a flat tire, am (allegedly) nagged by my wife, stub my toe, get bitten by my cat, or watch the Pittsburgh Pirates lose, I feel unhappy. Yet I feel joy pretty much all the time, even while those bad things are happening. Feeling happy is different from feeling joy. I am about two-thirds finished reading *Choose Joy Because Happiness Isn't Enough* by Kay Warren. She doles out an overdose of scripture, in my opinion, and claims the Bible to be the unquestionable 100 percent Word of God. That's fine for her, but I have my own set of beliefs. And you have your own too.

Nevertheless, she gets it right, in my view, much of the time throughout her book. She defines joy as "the settled assurance that God is in control of all the details of my life, the quiet confidence that ultimately everything is going to be all right, and the determined choice to praise God in all things."

I like that. Happiness, she claims, is a temporary state, while joy lasts for all time because joy can only be found through God. He is eternal and so is our joy. So what does all this have to do with alcoholism? Plenty. I have found joy, and with it comes sobriety. I am still learning how trusting my higher power works so much better at bringing joy than draining a bottle down my throat. There's a new sensation that comes from truly finding God and seeking to do his will.

"God has promised, repeatedly to care for us, reassuring us that he knows our needs even before we ask... When we refuse him—as evidenced by our tension headaches, chewed up fingernails, irritability, stomachaches, (drinking), and sleepless nights—we are saying, 'I know you were there in the past, but what about now? I'm not sure you can be counted on, God, so I had better figure this out on my own.'"

Refuse booze/choose God.

Sober day 77
No supportive family? Build one out of friends

I haven't blogged for a while because I have been camping. This past week was our annual family getaway. This year, we camped by Port Townsend along Lake Erie in Ohio. Each year, my family and in-laws, who were friends long before we joined them with our marriage, get together to camp someplace. To paraphrase a cliché, you can't choose your family, but you *can* choose your in-laws. I scored on both counts! I couldn't ask for better. None of my wife's family suffers with drinking problems that I know of. So what went wrong with me? Worrying about the past, which can't be altered, gets in the way of living for the moment. *This* moment only! What went wrong with me doesn't matter nearly so much as the fact I had nothing to drink today. Tomorrow can worry about tomorrow. This is the day and this is the moment in which I live.

If you aren't as lucky as I to have a supportive family, you need to depend on your sponsor, AA friends, workmates, church co-minglers, maybe a sober neighbor or two. Make them your family. But whatever you do, don't blame your addiction on growing up in a dysfunctional home. I'm sorry for that, but move on, embrace the Serenity Prayer. Don't blame Mom or Dad or that funny uncle who messed you up. It's a new day. How are you going to only live in today so that tomorrow can be even better? I don't mean that as a rhetorical question. How are you going to?

Sober day 78
Feeling pain? Don't choose booze

We store pains in our brains and issues in our tissues. Sounds to me like a good excuse to drink, huh? At least it was a good excuse for me. If you think too much, you may drink too much. "Go ahead, self-medicate," that evil little voice inside me used to say. Did it work? You know the answer already. If it did, my brain right now would be fogging, not blogging. My corpuscles would be clogging. I'm going to stop this rhyme, just in time (it sounds pretty stupid, and I don't want you to miss the point). That point is that alcohol is poison, bad medicine, addictive, and dangerous. To remove pain from your brain and issues from your tissues, try God, pray daily, take your higher power on vacation with you. He will fit in a carry-on. Your gray matter matters.

Sober day 79
Why is this the best of all possible worlds?

I can't remember whether it was in high school or college when I stumbled through the pages of *Candide*, an eighteenth century novel by Voltaire. I only remember this haunting sentence repeated over and over, when Candide confronts any horrific event: "All is for the best in this best of all possible worlds." That satirical refrain stuck with me, I guess, because I didn't know if I agreed with Candide's naivete or Voltaire's mockery of that philosophy. Take alcoholism, for example. The degradation of personality and health doesn't fit into a "best of all possible worlds." I felt embarrassed among friends and family and hated myself with a hatred I thought I could never forgive. Then I found God again. I believed I had found him every time before I relapsed, but the wicked voice inside me, tempting me, was stronger than God's. This current stretch of sobriety I am into feels much different.

For the first time, I understand what AA people mean when they refer to a "dry drunk." That was me, but I am different now. I understand my character defects so that I can turn them over to God and eliminate them. I understand others' suffering with addiction and feel in a better position to support them. When I speak at AA meetings, I can feel God speaking through me. Heck, I don't talk like that. Where in heaven's name are these words coming from? The question remains: Does everything happen "for the best in this best of all possible worlds?" My healing tells me it does. So then what about wars and murders and rapes and cheating and lying and stealing and death and fires and hurricanes and earthquakes, and the list goes on. I have come to believe that God uses bad stuff to make us better. Just as my alcoholism has made me a better person than I would be if I had never taken a drink. God leads us through such dark times.

Here is a good explanation. It comes from Rick Warren in *The Purpose Driven Life*

Our greatest lessons come out of pain, and the Bible says God keeps a record of our tears. Whenever problems occur, remember that God uses them to fulfill all five purposes in your life: Problems force you to focus on God, draw you closer to others in fellowship, build Christ-like character, provide you with a ministry, and give you a testimony. Every problem is purpose-driven.

See a video of Godspell's "Yes, It's All for the Best," which ironically closes with a view of the Twin Towers.

Sober day 80
I feel guilty, yes; shameful, I hope not

I did a lot of things as a drunk that leave me feeling guilty years later. For example, I—nope, don't want to get into that again. I can't allow my guilt to escalate into shame. So what's the difference? I wrote a quote in my book of notes. Someone at AA said, "Guilt is 'I made a mistake.' Shame is 'I *am* the mistake.'" Whoever said that summarized in one sentence what it took Brené Brown 285 pages to say in *I Thought It Was Just Me (But It Isn't)*. "Shame is the intensely painful feeling or experience of believing we are flawed and therefore unworthy of acceptance and belonging... Shame creates feelings of fear, blame and disconnection..." The good news, however, is that we are all capable of developing shame resilience. Again, by *resilience* I mean that ability to recognize shame when we experience it and move through it in a constructive way that allows us to maintain our authenticity and grow from our experiences.

And in this process of consciously moving through our shame, we can build stronger and more meaningful connections with the people in our lives. That's an important distinction between feelings of guilt and feelings of shame. I try not to allow myself to feel shame because "shame" isn't who I am. I want to remember the guilty feelings that came with my drinking, but I can't let my guilt define who I am. God loves me. My family loves me. I am worth it. I deserve their acceptance of who I am, flaws and all.

Sober day 81
Is addiction really a disease? Or am I just a dirtbag?

The debate rages: Is alcoholism a matter of choice or is it a disease? Well, maybe not "rages." But the question does go "blip" in some circles. My cousin, in a phone text, referenced a blog post I wrote on May 20 about the disease question, and she pointed me in the direction of a YouTube address by Dr. Kevin McCauley. It's well worth the investment of an hour, twelve minutes, and thirteen seconds for an easy-to-follow analysis of addiction and our brains.

The prefrontal cortex is the part of the brain that controls conscious thought, behavior, decision-making, and the like. Experiments with mice prove that's not where addiction attacks. The midbrain is the survival brain. It handles eating, killing (self-protection), and sex. This is the part of the brain where alcohol and other drugs work, which means we are tricked into believing we need more and more for survival. Nothing else then matters. We drink to live and live to drink. Some fortunates can drink or drug, and it's just fun. Then they stop, get over the hangover, and move on. For them, a beer is a beer.

But for addicts, a beer becomes life or death. The cause of addiction, according to McCauley, is stress. We all face stress, but we don't all face the same severity of stress (rape, abuse, natural disasters), the same pattern of stress (stress in early life is more damaging, stress to a fetus in the first trimester of pregnancy is toxic), the same coping mechanisms, or the same brains. "Addiction is a stress-induced defect in the brain's ability to properly perceive pleasure," McCauley says:

> If people can't properly perceive light, they are blind. No one judges them or takes away their children. If people can't perceive sound, they are

deaf and no one passes judgment against them for that. But those who can't perceive pleasure properly and seek it in different ways, (alcohol, drugs, sex, food) often are perceived as immoral or lacking control over themselves or having terrible parents or friends. That's certainly true for some alcoholics, but if so it's for reasons not tied to their drinking and drugging. Instead: Addiction is a dysregulation of the midbrain dopamine (pleasure) system due to unmanaged stress resulting in symptoms of decreased functioning, specifically:

1. Loss of control
2. Craving
3. Persistent drug use despite negative consequences.

So when folks face jail time or loss of their kids or threats from a spouse if they don't stop drinking, we would expect them to want to stop to avoid the consequences. Makes sense. *But threats have no effect on use. They add stress, which increases the likelihood of more substance abuse and relapse.* But don't take it from me. Listen to what Dr. McCauley has to say about the disease of addiction. It's good stuff (the words, I mean, not the disease).

Sober day 82
If you need help with that speck in your eye, allow me

I miss Jeff. We worked down the hall from each other until a brain tumor or something forced him to quit and move back home to western Pennsylvania. We graduated the same year from high school just a few miles apart, and both found our way to Rohm and Haas in Louisville. I visited him once at his home in Zelienople when he was sick. Not long after, I drove 450 miles to attend his funeral there. Jeff told me something I will always remember. The lesson seems clear to me now, but it took a while to sink in. My recovery from alcoholism has helped me hear his words more clearly. He stood in my office door one day and told me that what we say about other people tells more about us than it does about them. I don't remember how the conversation evolved to that point.

But he said, if we say someone is lazy, for example, that doesn't mean he is. That just means that we fear laziness in ourselves. If we say someone is boastful, the real reason we think so may be that he is stealing the spotlight from us and our own "braggadociosness" (do you like that word?). After all, he should get out of his self-made spotlight and give someone more deserving (like me?) a chance to shine. The Bible tells us to remove the plank from our own eye before we try to remove the speck in someone else's. The *Big Book*, in my favorite personal narrative in the back, uses sarcasm to deliver the same admonition. On page 417 of "Acceptance Is the Answer," it says:

> *Shakespeare said, "All the world's a stage, and all the men and women are merely players." He forgot to mention I was the chief critic. I was able to see the flaw in every person, every situation. And I was always glad to point it out, because I knew you wanted perfection, just as I did. AA and acceptance have taught me that there is a bit of good in the worst of us and a bit of bad in the best of us; that we are all children of God and we each have a right to be here.*

> Higher up on the same page, *"I can find no serenity until I accept that person, place, thing, or situation as being exactly the way it is supposed to be at this moment."*

Sobriety, I hope, is helping me see others as God's handiwork. What gives me the right to find fault in what God has made? AA meetings help remind me of this. Everyone in the rooms is different from me. Different, not better and not inferior. We all are fighting the same disease. We all are trying to get that splintery plank from our own eyes so we can accept others as they are, not as we think they should be.

Sober day 83
AA offers online groups

My uncle, my late father's only brother, passed away last year. I drove seven hours to Grove City, Pennsylvania, to say goodbye. I stayed with my mother for several days and decided to check out AA meetings in town. I was able to find a meeting three of the days I was there. Opportunities were limited in that small community. I was used to choosing from among four hundred-plus meetings every week in Louisville where I live. Just today, I discovered a new AA resource I hadn't been aware of. There is a series of online intergroup meetings you can join to fill in the gaps when you can't physically attend at a time and a place near you. You choose from available groups and sign up. I haven't tried that yet but would like to hear from someone who has. Do online intergroup meetings work for you? For a list of available groups to join, visit:

Sober day 84
Hear ye, hear ye! I made a confession

At last, I came out of the closet yesterday. No, not *that* closet. I have been married—to a woman—for forty-one years. *My* closet is filled with empties. I finally worked up the courage to tell my four hundred-plus Facebook friends that I am a recovering alcoholic. I shared the address of my blog in hopes of reaching more people who need to be reached. I received many positive responses so far. I feel like I am loved, even by people I went to school with and haven't seen in decades. Thank you, dear friends. If you, like me, have been timid about admitting an addiction problem, I would urge you to come clean, based on my experience. I figured if someone doesn't understand my disease and wants to pass judgment against me, that is no big loss. I pray for them and hope alcoholism never darkens their family's doorstep.

Sober day 86
I'm not the brightest bulb in the store

I heard a riddle at today's AA speakers meeting. How many alcoholics does it take to change a light bulb? One. He just holds it, and the world turns around him! I find that particularly humorous in light of one of my character defects I have identified and work to change every day: self-centeredness. According to Freud, "Whoever loves becomes humble. Those who love have, so to speak, pawned a part of their narcissism."

If I pawned my narcissism, I have yet to receive any cash for it, which suggests I am still hanging on to some of it. One day, I was found unresponsive on the floor in my house after a binge of over-indulgence. When I was lying in intensive care, a social worker told me about AA and gave me a list of local meetings. I told her thanks but no thanks. What I didn't tell her was that I knew the kind of people who attend AA meetings, and I'm not one of them. I have a college degree. I retired after being a professional for thirty-five years. I have a nice home and never have lived in a box under a bridge. I am happily married and have two successful, well-adjusted kids. I have flown all over the country and have been in forty-nine states. That's not the profile of an AA member. Just a minute. I am having trouble unscrewing this light bulb.

There is no one-description-fits-all in AA. I learned I am just like everyone else at meetings. We all are there for the same reason. God didn't make me special in any way. We all are special in some way. I know lots of people—good people—I wouldn't have known if not for AA. God led me there to help me dismount from my high horse. The *Big Book* explains on page 62:

> *Selfishness—self-centeredness! That, we think, is the root of our troubles. Driven by a hundred forms of fear, self-delusion, self-seeking, and self-pity, we step on the toes of our fellows and they retaliate. Sometimes they hurt us, seemingly without provocation, but we invariably find that at some time in the past we have made decisions based on self which later placed us in a position to be hurt.*

The earth doesn't revolve around me. I have to turn my wrist to change light bulbs.

Sober day 87
"Thy kingdom come, thy will be done," then it gets tricky

We pray the Lord's Prayer. We hold hands in a circle and repeat it after most AA meetings. We say it every Sunday in church. When I was little, we said it before each school day began (Yeah, in public school. Can you believe it?). But did you ever notice that there's a catch to it? Everything is asked straightforward: Give us our daily bread, don't lead us into temptation, deliver us from evil. Right in the middle is a scary action item for *us*, a do-this-for-me-and-I-will-do-this-for-you deal we make with God. "And forgive us our trespasses, as we forgive those who trespass against us." In the Presbyterian church where I grew up, we replace "trespasses" with "debts." I guess Presbyterians are more worried about money they owe and others owe them than they are about trespassing. Un-Presbyterians promise to obey God's "No Trespassing!" signs, the same as we forbid others from our own yards. But neither trespasses nor debts gets to the main issue here.

Don't we really mean "Forgive us our sins as we forgive those who sin against us?" Ah, but here's the rub! We ask God to forgive our sins, but only if we forgive all the schmucks that sin against us. I take that to mean anyone—*anyone*—who robs us, cheats us, punches us, calls us bad names, makes fun of our mothers, cuts us off in traffic, rapes our daughters, molests young boys, sells drugs at our workplaces, rolls their eyes at us. You can think of more.

We pray to God, "I want and need your forgiveness but only as much as I am willing to forgive other people." That can be a heavy burden around our necks. I struggle to forgive the hoods who broke into our house a few years ago and stole my wife's jewelry, most of which had sentimental value. Her great-grandma's necklace and her engagement ring are gone. Forever. The two perpetrators were caught and sent to jail and ordered to pay restitution. But no restitution can ever replace her stolen wedding ring.

God says I have to forgive them. In essence, I tell God not to forgive me unless I can forgive the burglars. It's hard, but I must do it. I have created far worse sins against God. I'm sorry, God, for all those things I did while drunk and sober. Forgive me, just as I forgive those sinners who broke the lock on my back door. In AA's Step 7, we humbly ask God to remove our shortcomings. We take it further in Step 8 when we list everyone we have harmed. Then in Step 9, we put ourselves out there and make amends to all those people.

I guess I simply have to do it. I have to forgive others, just the same as I want God to forgive me. I need to realize that God loves those burglars, just as much as he loves Mother Teresa. He expects me to do the same. So I forgive you guys, and ask that God turns your lives around, just as he has done for me when he steered me away from alcohol.

Sober day 88
I need to know what blew out my engine

Excuse me, but I disagree with something I just read. In the book *Staying Sober—A Guide for Relapse Prevention* by Terrence Gorski and Merlene Miller, the authors seem to be saying that why we drink doesn't matter. They say just attack the problem itself. "Searching for the cause of an addiction (such as emotional or family problems) is usually nonproductive. Treatment that recognizes the addiction as a primary condition rather than a symptom of something else has been found to be most effective."

I have a different perspective. My symptom is alcoholism. The disease isn't addiction to alcohol. It's self-centeredness, unfulfilled dreams, regrets, and other character defects. I need to understand the disease and work through the primary condition of that disease, so then I can eliminate the resulting symptom—alcoholism.

Let me draw an analogy. My car started going *kerlunk, kerlunk, kertwottle*. I couldn't solve the problem unless I knew the cause. Well, I never would figure out the cause unless I took it to an expert. The mechanic looked, diagnosed, and fiddled with the engine. At last, he said what it needed replaced. Once he found a new part, my car would be purring. And $237.59 later, he was right. My drinking is a parallel story. Understanding my addiction helps me control it. In my case, staying away from people imbibing didn't help. Hating myself didn't help. Counseling and AA helped, but I continued to relapse, nonetheless.

One of my "mechanics"—I'll call her Leslie (because that really is her name)—talked me through my relapses and helped me identify a pattern. I often drank before and after trips to visit family, weekends during football season, and daytimes after retirement when I was used to being at my job. I realized it was my happy past and boring present that led me to relapse. Leslie taught me techniques and referred me to readings designed to help me live in the moment. Living in the past was senseless, I learned, because nothing good or bad could be relived or unlived. That doesn't mean killing my memories. That's what I tried to do with alcohol.

Instead, I can reminisce about good times and people who have passed from this lifetime, but I don't live back then. I let those times go so I can stop missing *new* good times. I live for this moment because that's all I've got. That's all any of us have got. *Staying Sober* has many good points I *can* agree with. Here is one: "A life that includes wholesome living, uplifting relationships, commitment to values outside of oneself, and spiritual growth supports long-term health and sobriety."

Sober day 93
Don't be afraid of the dark

> *Showing others who suffer how we were given help is the very thing which makes life seem so worthwhile to us now. Cling to the thought that, in God's hands, the dark past is the greatest possession you have—the key to life and happiness for others. With it you can avert death and misery for them.* (The *Big Book*, page 124)

I am grateful for my dark past. No, I'm not masochistic. It's just that we learn more from our losses than from our victories. Fortunately, my dark past only goes back ten years or so, unlike many others I know who have been suffering since their teens. Yesterday, I received my green ninety-day token at my AA home group meeting! I've been here before but never with the joy I have discovered by staying sober this time around. If I hadn't driven through the dark past, I never would have come to know myself and how to repair the damage I caused to myself and others. Only because I had bad times did I find God and pray for his will to be done through me. I see results of that prayer every day.

When I lived in Idaho, I came to realize those beautiful mountains couldn't exist without valleys. A lack of valleys is what makes the Great Plains, plains. We need highs and lows to appreciate life or else our lives would look like North Dakota or someplace like that. My low came from drinking. My high comes from God. My dark past truly is the greatest possession I have. Rick Warren, in *The Purpose Driven Life*, says it this way: "The good news is that God wants you to pass the tests of life, so he never allows the tests you face to be greater than the grace he gives you to handle them."

Sober day 95
God may be found through Kermit's kinfolk

Tom at AA recently confessed. Not to a priest. Far from it. He admitted to us that he once was an agnostic. I keep getting agnostics confused with atheists. An agnostic is a person who holds the view that God is unknown and probably unknowable. An atheist doesn't believe in God or any gods. Period.

So back to Tom, who converted from agnosticism one day. He said he was at the club where AA meetings take place several times a day. He strolled behind the building to the large grass-and-tree-filled lot beyond the parking area. "God, do you exist?" He wanted to know. Just asking the question shows his heart was open to finding God. A higher power is essential to escaping alcoholism. See Step 2.

Tom stood and listened. "I heard a frog. Then another. Then I heard lots of frogs. I came back to the meeting and told them, 'I found God. He is a frog!'" At a later meeting, I remember someone saying FROG stands for "Fully Rely on God."

Many of us find God in nature. I don't think he *is* nature, but he can certainly be found there. Tom doesn't worship frogs, but he found a higher power through a *ribbit*. Where you find God doesn't matter as long as you keep your ears, eyes, and heart open to him. The *Big Book*, on page 397, says, *"In fact, I did not need to find God. I only needed an open mind, and the spirit found me."*

Sober day 96
What have you done for you lately?

I know them, and you know them too: those Bible-thumping, scripture-quoting, righteous-feeling people. Some of them talk the talk without walking the walk.

The last time I went to church religiously (pun intended), I became disillusioned when the new pastor, a righteous-feeling married man, resigned in disgrace after an affair with a woman in the church. We've become nauseated by a stream of reports through the years of priests molesting underaged boys. Did they think God was napping when they committed these atrocities? Right or wrong, I confess I expect more from men—and women—of the cloth.

I hear a few people at AA meetings quoting *Big Book* passages but doing nothing. Are they living those passages or grandstanding? Cynthia said at my home group meeting that she knew a man who attended AA meetings for twenty years but did nothing for AA, other members, or his own sobriety. He died drunk.

"Faith without works is dead" (*Big Book*, page 88). The Daily Reflection for February 15 reads:

> One of the most important things AA has given me, in addition to freedom from booze, is the ability to take "right action." It says the promises will always materialize if I work for them. Fantasizing about them, debating them, preaching about them, and faking them just won't work. I'll remain a miserable, rationalizing dry drunk.

None of us are perfect, for sure, but we can all try harder.

Sober day 97
When you own a mistake, promptly admit it

We must take ownership of our actions. As Mark said at AA, "The cookie broke. No, say, 'I broke the cookie.'" Step 10 tells us: *"Continued to take personal inventory and when we were wrong promptly admitted it."* That takes me back to junior high English class and to my many years as a journalist and corporate writer. Don't use passive voice if you know the subject of the sentence. Use active voice. Example: "The boy followed his dog into the woods," not "The dog was followed by the boy into the woods." Say, "Thieves broke into the house," not "The house was broken into by thieves." Likewise, not "The beer was drunk," but "I drank the beer (and now I am drunk)."

I need to take ownership of my actions. And when I am wrong, promptly admit it.

Sober day 98
Don't pass up the smorgasbord

I'll give Tom somebody-or-other credit for today's verbal feast. He said AA meetings are like a buffet with prime rib and lobster and lots more good things. Some come in and take a carrot or a piece of celery, and then they leave. You wonder why they can't see all the delicious yummies they are leaving behind.

I did that for a while—just took a whiff and moved on. I didn't know what lobster is or what prime rib tastes like, so a leaf of lettuce seemed just fine. My words of wisdom today, thanks to Tom, are to try a bite of sobriety, just for today. Don't worry about tomorrow. When tomorrow comes, taste sobriety once more, just for the new today, and so on. You get the idea. Staying sober isn't easy until you find out how good it tastes.

Sober day 99
"Yes, we have no bananas"

This comes from Paul—sober but clearly still working at it: "I've got the monkey off my back, but the circus is still in town."

Sober day 100
What counts is the pain of the sin, not the size

This is another Markism from my home group meeting. He heard of someone who admitted to stealing a piece of bubblegum. "I stole a case of whiskey," he said, "and he's worried about a piece of gum!"

But if that transgression bothered him, he was right to confess it when he did Step 5. That step doesn't do us much good if we hold back. Come clean. Confess it all. Step 5: *"Admitted to God, to ourselves, and to another human being the exact nature of our wrongs."* Step 5 should leave us ready for Step 6: *"Were entirely ready to have God remove all these defects of character."*

Sober day 101
Lift up your low self-esteem

I feel myself today wallowing in self-pity like a hog in mud, only without so much pleasure. It does me no good to feel that way. After all, I'm the only one attending my pity party. Maybe. But there are times I am afraid my family hates me for all I did to myself and to them. I need to step back and change how I'm feeling about myself.

Despite it all, my wife didn't leave me. My kids still come around and go to dinner with me, help me around the house, and even go camping with us sometimes. My family stuck through everything with me. That should tell me they think I'm worth it. So get over that self-flagellation! I'm not such a bad person after all.

Sober day 103
Mining quotes from the depths of AA and Thomas Merton

Here are some gems from AA meetings I found to be worth digging up:

"Choices and reactions are the only things we have control over."
"The more I know, the less I know."
"What if someone said, 'I am going to control your life'? I would say no way! But that's what I allowed alcohol to do."
"Sometimes I wish my brain had put the brakes on my mouth."
"People at AA poked me in the I."
"When I drink, I break out in stupid."
At New Year's: "I let my resolutions go in one year and out the other."
"Poor me! Pour me another."
EGO—Edging God Out.
"Religion is different spokes on the same wheel" (attributed to Thomas Merton).
"Give up the high cost of low living."

Sober day 109
From my pedestal, I could look down on you

I was in Grove City, Pennsylvania, visiting my mother, my sister, and her family the past two days. At lunch yesterday, my sister made the observation that I had been placed on a pedestal and that made me judgmental. There was a time I would have bristled and denied her opinion. My mother's nods, anyway, added oomph to her statement. I never thought I was on any pedestal. But my healing from alcoholism did make me acknowledge in Step 4 that I was full of myself, and I found characteristics in many others that I judged made them inferior. Yes, I'm afraid I have been judgmental.

My sister and mother went on to agree that I'm not as bad at that as I used to be. I hope that is so. The Twelve Steps made me come to the realization that everyone is just like me—none better, none inferior. Praise God for turning my alcoholism into positive acknowledgments of my old self. I turn my character defects over to God. Make me a better person, I pray.

Sober day 110
Heard any good numbers lately?

Have you been there before? Sitting on the same barstool, talking and listening to the same tired stories, over and over, night after night. You'd all laugh together, yet you think you're the only one depressed and miserable. Then a new fellow enters the bar. He orders a bourbon, of course, because this is Kentucky. A young man off in the corner shouts, "Fifteen!" Everyone laughs and goes on drinking. So do you, until a tired-looking old man at the bar, in a slurred voice, cries out, "Ninety-four!" Do you laugh? Sure, you do, because everyone else does. You've been here with them often.

The stranger looks perplexed. "Forty-seven!" comes a voice from somewhere. Everyone roars with laughter, then sips another sip.

"Why do these people shout numbers, and why do people laugh?" he asked.

The poor woman next to you lifts her head off the bar. "We all have heard the same stories and the same jokes so many times that the man in that booth over there assigned numbers. Now we just say the numbers. We all know what we mean. These are some really funny jokes." She lays her head back on the bar.

The newcomer orders another bourbon and then, with a grin, calls, "Sixty-one!" No one laughs. "Is sixty-one a bad joke?"

The woman drowsily lifts up her head again. "No," she said. "That's a good one. You just didn't tell it right."

Sober day 111
We are living in "The Age of Miracles"

"Do you believe in miracles?" Al Michaels was talking about the US team of young amateur boys beating the professional Russian soldiers in Olympic hockey in the 1980 Olympics. How about you? Do *you* believe in miracles? A pickup truck often parked at my home group AA meetings has a bumper sticker that says simply, "Miracles Happen." I'm a miracle. And so are you. Page 153 of the *Big Book* says:

> *It may seem incredible that these men are to become happy, respected, and useful once more. How can they arise out of such misery, bad repute, and hopelessness? The practical answer is that since these things have happened among us, they can happen with you. Should you wish them above all else, and be willing to make use of our experience, we are sure they will come. The age of miracles is still with us. Our own recovery proves that!*

I never heard a burning bush speak, changed water into wine, or brought life to the dead, but I *have* seen miracles. They come in the form of little things: a child recovers from cancer, a passenger in an auto rollover walks away. I find the seemingly right words to comfort an alcoholic who has relapsed umpteen times. I see another miracle in the mirror every day I abstain from alcohol. Look for miracles. They are all around you. For each one you witness, thank God and ask that his will be done.

Sober day 112
"As you trudge the road to happy destiny"

What if I were out with a group of friends? I never hung out in bars, so let's say I am on a trail in the woods with the hiking group I have trekked with before. One of them introduces me to someone new. We lag at the back of the pack, talking sports and hobbies and interests. After we spend time together, this man I thought was a friend suddenly sneers, "I am going to control your life!"

What would you do in a similar situation? Would you agree to meet after the hike to see what he means? Would you scoff and tell yourself you never would agree to something so ridiculous? Would you distance yourself from this awful person? Or maybe you would say, "Sure! While you're at it, I will divorce my wife, give up my kids, leave my job, and enable you to be my higher power."

You can see what I am getting at. I made friends with alcohol and let it control my life. How stupid I was! I made a mistake. I lost money and self-esteem to enable—actually invite—alcohol to control my life.

In time, I escaped that hiker's clutches, kicked him out of my life, accepted a new higher power I call God, and found another hiking group. You can too. It is never too late.

Sober day 113
God, take the wheel before I crash

I can't be in control all the time. There were times I wanted to be, tried to be, demanded I be. That never worked out so hot. I came up with an analogy once when on a trip. The pilot, crew, and control tower were in control, not me. That's a situation where I *had* to relinquish all control and trust others. My record as a pilot wasn't so good.

I also noted that, for many years, in the car, I have been riding in the passenger seat. My wife is at the wheel. She likes to drive, and I would rather look at the scenery. On longer trips, I read and nap as she drives. I trust her to get us where we are going safely. Sometimes I offer suggestions: "Don't follow so close behind that truck;" "Pass the old lady in front of us;" "The light is changing;" "Cars are stopping ahead." She rarely takes my suggestions. She is in control and would rather do things her own way. I am better off keeping my mouth shut and turning up the radio (that's a suggestion she firmly offers to me).

Likewise, it hasn't been easy letting God control my life. I had better ideas and tried to make suggestions but to no avail. Then I came to Step 3: *Made a decision to turn our will and our lives over to the care of God as we understood him.* When I gave up control of my life and finally trusted God to fly the plane for me, life became easier. I was less stressed. Good things happened. Problems got solved. *I stopped drinking.* And when I felt as if I were being tested, I prayed and let God give me the answers. Only then did I get straight As.

Sober day 114
Looking for love in all the wrong places

I'm married, happily so. Today's words of wisdom don't apply to me. But if you are a recovering alcoholic and have yet to collect your one-year metal token, think about this. I have heard and read a number of times that it's a bad idea to hook up with someone romantically until you are at least one year sober. Alcoholics' brains aren't ready for a commitment yet. First you have to stay concerned with your sobriety. A love interest and the emotional strain it brings can lead to drinking away stress or maybe drinking in celebration of your new love. We alcoholics can make up too many reasons to drink again. So try this. Start with a plant, a potted plant. Whether it blooms or withers, accept it. Next, try a goldfish. Feed it, nurture it, flush it when it dies. Then get another.

Someday you will be ready to try a dog or a cat. Feel the love and love it back. Maybe by this point, you won't be drawn to the opposite sex or maybe you will. There are just some things you can't get from a cat. But if you have learned to nurture a plant, a fish, and a mammal, and you are more than a year into your recovery, maybe then you are ready for companionship of the human kind.

Just don't rush into anything. Staying sober should be the most important priority in your life.

Sober day 116
Shut out inner noisemakers and trust your guts

Women's panel talk shows, news debates, and sports shows filling the gap between halves of a ball game all annoy me. Participants all think they have something to say, and they say it loudly, over the voices of others. "Hear me! I am right, and, furthermore, what I have to say is witty."

When I face choices between actions I should follow, my brain erupts in a similar shouting match. Eventually, I come to hush the cacophony and sort through the voices to make a decision. Call it a hunch. Call it intuition. Call it a feeling, a sense. Call it the voice of God. No matter what you call it, I come to learn which inner voice to listen to. How about you?

Which voice is God's will and which voice is mine, trying to outshout God? I find the best way to receive and carry out the right message, the solution to God's test, is to step back, take a couple days off, maybe a week. When I do that, I can act with more confidence I am following God's will. I ace his test! But not if I let the loudest inner voice get in my way. You know, that's how I kept relapsing. A drink will make me feel better and help me make the right choice, I thought. The more drinks, the more I am sure I am right. That was me talking, but my gut was trying to tell me something else. How stupid of me! I needed to wait a day, wait a week. Your heart will lie to you. Your mind will lie to you. But your gut never lies. That gut feeling, I think, is the voice of God. Listen and follow it.

Sober day 117
You can't stress for success

Once in a while, as part of do-it-myself therapy, I go through old papers and brochures I collected through inpatient and outpatient treatment. I ran across one about stress I thought I ought to share. I don't know who to give credit to for this, so excuse me for plagiarizing. Actually, I'm putting it into my own words, so it's not exactly plagiarism, is it? Whoever wrote this, I trust you would be glad if the words will be helpful to someone. I'm going to spread your ten stress-reduction techniques out over the next five days.

Stress-reduction techniques

Meditate. I have trouble turning off my brain to meditate effectively. "Research suggests that daily meditation may alter the brain's neural pathways, making you more resilient to stress," according to psychologist Robbie Maller Hartman, a Chicago health and wellness coach. Try this:

> Sit up straight with both feet on the floor.
> Close your eyes and focus on reciting—out loud
> or silently—a positive mantra such as "I feel at
> peace" or "I love myself."

What helps me to meditate is to do a search of YouTube. I find useful stuff that helps me block out my thoughts and focus on my meditation.

Breathe deeply. Take a five-minute break when you feel troubles and focus on your breathing instead. Slowly inhale through your nose until your lungs are full. Then slowly exhale through your mouth. Deep breathing can also be an important part of your meditation. "Deep breathing counters the effects of stress by slowing the heart rate and lowering blood pressure," says psychologist Judith Tutin, a certified life coach in Rome, Georgia.

Sober day 118
You can't stress for success (continued) stress-reduction techniques

Be present. Slow down. What's your hurry? I'm really bad at this, especially in the car. I push the speedometer ahead a couple MPH, then a couple more, even if there's no reason to get to where I'm going ninety seconds or so faster. "Take five minutes and focus on only one behavior with awareness," says life coach and psychologist Dr. Judith Tutin. Notice how the air feels on your face when you open the car window or walk and how your feet feel hitting the ground. Enjoy the texture and flavor of each bite of food you chew. When you spend time living in the moment and focusing on your senses, you should feel the tension leaving your body.

Reach out. A good social support system is an important way to deal with stress. That's a key benefit I get from attending AA meetings. Talking to people helps defuse stressful feelings.

Sober day 119
You can't stress for success (continued) stress-reduction techniques

Tune into your body. Be aware of yourself. Perform a mental scan of your body. Start with your toes and work your way up to your head, noticing how your body feels. "Simply be aware of places you feel tight or loose without trying to change anything," Dr. Tutin advises. "For one or two minutes, imagine each deep breath flowing to that body part. Repeat the process, paying close attention to sensations you feel in each body part."

Decompress. Place a warm heat wrap around your neck and shoulders for ten minutes. Close your eyes and relax your face, neck, upper chest, and back muscles. I can accomplish the same thing in a warm shower. I suppose a bath would work too.

Sober day 120
You can't stress for success (continued) stress-reduction techniques

Laugh out loud. I like this one. A funny movie or TV show helps me relax. You might not like my kind of humor, but give *Young Frankenstein* a try. I love *Police Squad* episodes, *Naked Gun* movies, *Airplane* and *Airplane II*. I laugh, even when I know what line is coming next. A good laugh lowers cortisol, your body's stress hormone, while surely increasing brain pleasure chemicals called endorphins. But don't call me Shirley.

Crank up the tunes. Research shows that listening to soothing music can lower blood pressure, heart rate, and anxiety. "Create a playlist of songs or nature sounds (the ocean, a bubbling brook, birds chirping) and allow your mind to focus on the different melodies, instruments, or singers in the piece," suggests Cathy Benninger, a nurse at The Ohio State University Wexner Medical Center. You should be able to find some sounds that help if you search YouTube. Try a bunch of different things and see what works for you.

Sober day 121
You can't stress for success (continued) stress-reduction techniques

Get moving. You don't have to run in order to get a runner's high, but do run if you can. That sure worked for me in my younger days. All forms of exercise, including yoga and good old-fashioned walking, can ease depression and lower anxiety by helping the brain release feel-good chemicals. Yes, they're the same feel-good chemicals released by drinking and drugging, but this "high" is good for you.

1. Take a walk round the block or through a park. My neighborhood has two lakes I enjoy walking around. Take the stairs instead of the elevator, park at the far end of the parking lot (as long as it's safe there), or do some simple exercises like head rolls and shoulder shrugs.

2. Be grateful. Try keeping a gratitude journal to help you remember all the things that are good in your life. God has given you plenty. Write it all down during your good times.

3. You can track pleasant things like raindrops on roses or whiskers on kittens or a child's smile, a sunny day, a compliment from a coworker, a new skill. When you start feeling stressed, spend a few minutes looking through your notes to remind yourself what really matters.

Sober day 123
Where there is his will, you will find a way

Pennsylvania, where I was born and raised, calls itself the Keystone State because people believed that, like a keystone, Pennsylvania held the other twelve states/colonies together.

Today's AA Daily Reflection calls Step 3 the keystone step. (*We made a decision to turn our will and our lives over to the care of God as we understood Him.*) "The 'other pieces' are Steps 1, 2, and 4 through 12. In one sense, this sounds like Step 3 is the most important Step, that the other eleven depend on the third for support. In reality, however, Step 3 is just one of the twelve. It is the keystone."

Without Step 3, no full recovery from alcoholism can be made. I think that is right. Turning our will and our lives over to the care of God or to our higher power is essential to recovery. It also is essential to the lives of *everybody*, alcoholic or addict or not. Trust God, follow his will. You will find that life is better that way. He knows what is best for our lives.

Sober day 124
Thank you, humans! Thank you, God!

"That's gratitude for ya!"
I've heard that a lot and maybe said it myself at least once or ninety-nine times. These days, I am working on not expecting grati-

tude. If I go out of my way for someone, I do it out of love and caring, not recognition. The other side of this nickel is being sure to express *my* gratitude to others, even for the little things. When someone lets me out into the traffic flow, I wave my gratitude. I was treated to lunch today, and I certainly thanked my host. If you read my first entry to this blog, you will see that I lost my gratitude to God. I expected him to go easy on me.

Kansas sang, "I was soaring ever higher, but I flew too high." That was me. I forgot it wasn't my brains or beauty that made my life so comfortable. It was God. I lost a lot from those days past, including my sobriety. Now I thank God for sun when it's sunny, rain when it's raining, and a day of sobriety when I don't drink. One AA Daily Reflection finishes: "When I remember my gratitude list, it's very hard to conclude that God is picking on me."

Sober day 125
With God as director, the show can go on

Abe comes to our noontime AA meetings once in a while. He is a big, strong-looking guy with a "preacher-esque" voice. At one meeting, he confided about Step 3, "I was willing to turn my life over to the care of God, but I was afraid to give it up." That's the antithesis of the driver who says, "Here. You steer for a while. I'm gonna take a nap."

Page 62 of the *Big Book* should be helpful to all you Abes out there who struggle with turning their lives over to a higher power, and it says:

> *First of all, we had to quit playing God. It didn't work. Next, we decided that hereafter in this drama of life, God was going to be our Director. He is the Principal; we are His agents. He is the Father, and we are His children. Most good ideas are simple, and this concept was the* keystone *(see Sober day 123 about keystones) of the new and triumphant arch through which we passed to freedom.*

This step isn't easy. How can we trust an invisible spirit to take all control? On page 63 is a prayer worth praying. Say it often and consider seriously its meaning. I will print it here, but I am changing the King James language used in the *Big Book,* and it states:

> *God, I offer myself to You—to build with me and to do with me as you will. Relieve me of the bondage of self, that I might better do Your will. Take away my difficulties so that victory over them will show others Your power, Your love, and Your way of life. May I always do Your will.*

Sober day 127
Making dry spells last—one day at a time

Sometimes it's good to step back and listen to the thoughts of other recovering alcoholics. Here is one that came to me on Facebook yesterday, and it says:

> There is such a huge difference between dry and sober. There were so many times during my drinking career that I would take a month off or "stop" drinking just so I could shut people up. Most of that time was spent dreaming about my next drink or wondering how long I had to make this dry spell last before people left me alone.
>
> When I finally got *sober* it was life changing. Sobriety and Recovery is a daily process filled with growth, forgiveness, spirituality, hope, love and so many other amazing things. I always say that if the rest of the world just lived by our principles the world would be such a better place.
>
> I'm so thankful to be sober and not dry. I've met many a "sober" person who is completely miserable because they're simply not drinking. If you are going to be miserable then what's the point?

Sober day 128
Mining precious gems with Dottie

I like Dottie. She is a member of my AA Let's Get Serious home group. Age seventy-something, eleven years sober, she comes up with some real gems. For example:

"(My kids) don't like where I came from, but they like where I came."

"I was like a person standing at the bus stop, but the bus doesn't go by there anymore."

"When I drink, I break out in stupid."

"The truth will set you free, but it might piss you off first."

"Keep coming back. Either you'll get it or it will get you."

"The worst thing that ever happened to me never did."

While I was looking back in my notebook for more Dottie-isms, I came across something the late Cecil said at a meeting in 2015: "AA isn't a religious program. Religion is for people trying to get to heaven. AA is a spiritual program for people who have been to hell and don't want to go back."

Sober day 136
It's one small step for us, one giant leap for God

I want to point something out about the relationship between two of AA's Twelve Steps. First, Step 3: *"Made a decision to turn our will and our lives over to the care of God as we understood Him."* Then, Step 11: *"Sought through prayer and meditation to improve our conscious contact with God as we understood Him, praying only for knowledge of His will for us and the power to carry that out."*

Step 3 makes me think of meeting a new friend and asking him to do something for me. "Take over my will and my life, please." By Step 11, I know this friend better, and now I'm willing to do something nice for him. "Hey, you know, I would be happy to spend more time with you, and if you want me to do something for you, just let me know what your will for me is." Step 11 strikes me as being a follow-up to Step 3. After Steps 4–10, I have come to know God better, and my hope is to do his will for me. Before the steps, I was messing up my life. By Step 11, I became eager to do God's will instead of my own.

The 12 Steps are a hard journey. Come take the trip with me and turn your life over to God. You will be amazed.

Sober day 141
If a tree is planted today, does it make a sound tomorrow?

The Daily Reflection of AA for March 29 leaves me unsure. After all, I am older now and my days are numbered. Well, my days *always* have been numbered, but it's a much smaller number now. This is what the Daily Reflection said:

> In Zorba the Greek, Nikos Kazantzakis describes an encounter between his principal character and an old man busily at work planting a tree. "What is it you are doing?" Zorba asks. The old man replies: "You can see very well what I'm doing, my son, I'm planting a tree." "But why plant a tree," Zorba asks, "if you won't be able to see it bear fruit?" And the old man answers: "I, my son, live as though I were never going to die." The response brings a faint smile to Zorba's lips and, as he walks away, he exclaims with a note of irony: "How strange—I live as though I were going to die tomorrow!"

So how am I supposed to live? As if I will live forever or as if this is my last day? If I am going to live forever, I can plant all the trees I want with assurance I will see them bear fruit. If I die tomorrow, I need to be sure I cross every T today and make all my amends (Step 9). I will live my last day as if nothing matters, because to me, it doesn't. Yeah, but to someone else, it *does* matter if I'm planting trees today. People later can enjoy the taste of fruit from my labors. I can plant goodwill and pay it forward so others can benefit from the harvest. Every tree planted will help somebody later. Whether I am still around to enjoy it or not, I am glad I could share.

Sober day 145
Walk this (straight) way

Jody relapsed the other night. She confessed tearfully at AA yesterday. It's not the first time she wept at a meeting. I can see she tries hard, but she is in the deadly clutches of that monster most of us battle as we try to stop drinking. Several times, in several ways, others at the meeting consoled her by pointing out that when we slip or relapse, we never lose what we gained. We have acquired new knowledge, new people, and new understanding of ourselves. Jody is better off now than during her last relapse because she has resources she didn't have before.

She now must recover from guilt, shame, and remorse. It's a hard road back. But at some point, that road straightens for us as long as we really want it to. Plus accepting God and his will for us will keep us on that straight road despite a few bumps and potholes.

Sober day 149
It's not easy being green when you're gray

I must face the facts: I am getting old. I used to consider most people I saw as "about my age." Reality is that we baby boomers are aging and dying off. I wrote down a note someone said at AA not long ago: "When you're ripe, you rot. When you're green, you grow." The trick is to see myself as green and growing. I am too healthy to turn ripe and rot.

I met with an orthopedic doctor yesterday. My knees have been bad for a long time, likely from running all those marathons and other races. He said my right knee, which had arthroscopic surgery fifteen years ago to remove damaged cartilage, was rubbing bone on bone. He couldn't understand how I could possibly still be running on it. My other knee has been sore because of a calcium deposit. He gave me a shot of cortisone in each knee and told me I never should run again.

I won't follow that order if I am away from home and away from my low-impact exercise equipment. I need to work out. Being unable to run without pain was one of the several factors that led me to abuse alcohol. If I return to a regimen of running and drinking, I will become ripe fruit about to rot. I'm not rotten fruit! God isn't finished with me. So with my green, sober life, I can continue to grow in other ways. This life of mine keeps getting better. Excuse me while I go walk the neighborhood.

Sober day 150
How did that elephant get in the room?

> There's a phrase, "the elephant in the living room," which purports to describe what it's like to live with a drug addict, an alcoholic, an abuser. People outside such relationships will sometimes ask, "How could you let such a business go on for so many years? Didn't you see the elephant in the living room?" And it's so hard for anyone living in a more normal situation to understand the answer that comes closest to the truth; "I'm sorry, but it was there when I moved in. I didn't know it was an elephant; I thought it was part of the furniture." There comes an aha-moment for some folks—the lucky ones—when they suddenly recognize the difference.
> —Stephen King

Sober day 152
Lose a friend, lose an addiction?

Todd has a concern. He is in the early phase of battling his addiction. His best friend of many years continues to use with no desire to stop. At AA today, Todd asked for guidance on whether he should drop his friend to keep himself clean or face temptation while holding on to the friend. I spoke up about page 101 in the *Big Book*:

> *In our belief any scheme of combating alcoholism which proposes to shield the sick man from temptation is doomed to failure. If the alcoholic tries to shield himself he may succeed for a time, but he usually winds up with a bigger explosion than ever. We have tried these methods. These attempts to do the impossible have always failed... Be sure you are on solid spiritual ground... Do not think of what you will get out of the occasion. Think of what you can bring to it.*

Dottie added this opposing viewpoint: "If you hang around a barbershop long enough, you're going to get a haircut."

Sober day 159
Set me free of my disease

Tell me if the lyrics of this popular song sound like alcoholism. That may not be what was intended, but it sounds like it could be to me.

"Disease"—Matchbox Twenty

I got a disease deep inside of me,
Makes me feel uneasy, baby
I can't live without you,
Tell me what am I supposed to do about it.
Keep your distance from it,
Don't pay no attention to me.
I got a disease.

I think that I'm sick.
But leave me be while my world is coming down on me.

You taste like honey, honey, tell me can I be your honey?
Be, be strong, keep telling myself that it won't take long till
I'm free of my disease, yeah free of my disease.
Set me free of my disease.

Sober day 160
First down and ten shots to go

It's October, and although the leaves haven't started changing here yet, summer is quickly becoming fall. That means football. I began my professional life as a sportswriter, even before I graduated from high school. I liked sports and I liked writing. What better way to spend adulthood? I worked part-time in a newspaper sports department through my college years, but for reasons best left to another blog entry, I got a different kind of reporting job after college. I continued life as a sports fan anyway.

When I was a kid, college football on Saturdays consisted of a doubleheader on the ABC network in the afternoon. That was all. We are in a new era now when games start at noon and continue well past midnight on the East Coast. There are so many games on so many channels, I have to print out the TV listings from my online newspaper so I can choose the games of most interest. Okay, so here's the point of this. I don't have any friends to invite over for twelve hours or so of football on TV. My wife, Kathy, works at the Louisville Zoo, which means weekends in October she usually works 2:00–10:30 at trick or treat there, the so-called "world's largest Halloween party."

For I don't know how many years, I thought the best way to take in all that football alone was to drink my way through it. Eventually, I didn't care who won or even who was playing. By the time my wife got home, I usually didn't remember any of it anyway. I was comfortably blacked out, asleep in my chair. I was sorry when I saw recaps of exciting finishes and vowed to watch sober next week. Of course, I didn't. After Halloween at the zoo was over, I continued drinking on weekends and weekdays. I just had to be more secretive about it. Football on TV was a trigger for me.

What triggers do you have? Rainy days? Sunny days? Snowstorms? Soap operas? Sad movies? Identify your weak moments and then have a plan to get past your trigger points without succumbing to them. For me, a prescription of Antabuse worked. So far. Drinking with Antabuse will make me sick, so I don't do it. I still watch football most of the day by myself. I find it to be a brain exercise to remember as many winners and losers as I can. By Monday, I forget a lot of scores, but that's because of my aging brain, not booze. That's okay. I now can enjoy a good football game sober.

Sober day 162
Two drugs society sadly tolerates—and more quotations

- "If you want to understand a society, take a good look at the drugs it uses. And what can this tell you about American culture? Well, look at the drugs we use. Except for pharmaceutical poison, there are essentially only two drugs that Western civilization tolerates: Caffeine from Monday to Friday to energize you enough to make you a productive member of society, and alcohol from Friday to Monday to keep you too stupid to figure out the prison that you are living in." (Bill Hicks)
- "Two ding-a-lings don't make a bell." (Denise, AA speaker)
- "Boredom is when all I'm thinking about is me." (Jim at a Louisville AA meeting)
- "AA is our gift *from* God. What we do with it is our gift *to* God." (Unknown)
- "How do you keep an idiot in suspense? I'll tell you later." (Greg at noon AA)
- "If you grow up in an abusive family, how do you ever learn how to love? Or do you? And how do you accept love from another?" (Danny, I think)
- "If you don't want a broken heart, pretend you don't have one." (Eddie)

- "If it's good, it's good. If it's bad, it's experience." (James)
- "A *Big Book* that is falling apart is likely owned by someone who isn't." (From a laminated sheet at an AA meeting)

Sober day 163
Am I a victim or a villain?

Victims can't recover. I heard that at AA last week and at first didn't know what it meant. Then I looked back at myself. I was a victim. My job was eliminated. My wife was down on me. My daughter quit speaking to me. I was lonely. Everyone was out to make my life miserable. I didn't deserve that, I thought.

See? I was a victim. As Larry said at AA, half my brain puts out BS and the other half buys it. For a time, I couldn't have stopped drinking, even if I had wanted to because my brain was buying my own BS.

Eventually, fortunately, I saw I was villain, not victim. I brought all the negative feelings on myself. No one was out to make me miserable. I did it to myself in the way I reacted to negative life events. So I changed myself and my approach to my alcohol addiction. No one could restore me to sanity—only God and myself. Voilà! My life changed. That's why I now say, "Victims can't recover."

Sober day 165
Where some of the people know your name

I enjoyed watching *Cheers*, and I still enjoy the reruns. It didn't occur to me until I learned about being alcoholic that it was unlikely that Sam, an alcoholic, could work in a bar he owned and serve drinks to others. Well, maybe he could after all. Jim said at AA that he used to work at a liquor store. "It was like a monkey working at a banana farm."

Take a look at page 468 in the AA *Big Book*, and it states:

> *I was allowing others to control my sense of*
> *well-being and behavior. I came to understand that*
> *the behavior, opinions, and thoughts of others were*

none of my business. The only business I was to be
concerned with was my own! I asked my Higher
Power to remove from me everything that stood in
the way of my usefulness to Him and others, and to
help me build a new life.

I suppose, with an attitude like that, one could tend bar or work in a liquor store or grow bananas without giving in to temptation. We need to look forward and not dwell on our mistakes of the past. The rearview mirror is small, but the windshield is large. Don't look back.

Sober day 167
"Someone you never met before"

A man who drinks too much on occasion is still the same man as he was sober. An alcoholic, a real alcoholic, is not the same man at all. You can't predict anything about him for sure except that he will be someone you never met before. (Raymond Chandler, *The Long Goodbye*)

Sober day 168
The past is never really over

We will not regret the past nor wish to shut the door on it. (AA Promises)

I've listened to insights on this promise at AA meetings many times, and I struggle with it. To not regret the past. That's a tough one. I did many things when I was drinking, and I sure as heck regret them. I think, if only I could turn back time and make different choices, my life would be better now. What my sponsor, Danny, says on the subject is useful:

We may regret things we did, but those things made us who we are now. There are lots of things we would do differently, if we could go back. All we can do is learn from those mistakes and never repeat them.

What if I never drank? What if my family had never lost faith in me? What if I had never met some people I thought were my friends? What if? As my sponsor said, those what-ifs are what made me the person I am. If I had never fallen victim to alcohol, I wouldn't be writing this blog, and you wouldn't be reading it. If anything I have written or will write is helpful to you in battling your own demons, it means maybe something positive has come from my past. I can't undo what I did, but I can make sure those rotten deeds will turn into something good. I can't let regret get the better of me.

Look at it this way. Do you know who Roberto Clemente was? He played right field for the Pittsburgh Pirates when I was growing up. He not only was a talented ball player, but he also hit and caught and threw with a flare you had to see to believe. He was Puerto Rican in a time when Latin American players weren't part of Major League Baseball. He loved kids and he loved Puerto Rico. He created countless opportunities for young boys whose lives he changed.

All that ended on New Year's Eve, 1972. An earthquake and a corrupt government in Nicaragua were keeping needed aid from reaching the people there. So he loaded a plane himself with supplies. He *over*loaded a plane with supplies. The plane crashed into the ocean a short time after taking off from Puerto Rico. Clemente's body was never found. I cried. I still do sometimes. If Clemente could regret his past, would he? Would he go back in time and cancel his plans that night? After all, none of those supplies ever made it to earthquake victims. But in Clemente's honor, people donated money and goods, many times more than the stuff that was on that plane. So was Clemente's crash a good thing or a flight of regret? In addition, ever since the crash, one of the greatest awards in baseball is the Roberto Clemente Award. Each team nominates a player who exemplifies Clemente's spirit of giving back to others. The award is an incentive to major leaguers who might otherwise not throw themselves into community service the way my childhood hero did.

An air disaster became an inspiration to many to serve others with compassion. If he could, would Clemente regret the past, regret loading that plane too full? It's impossible to say. But there is some consolation in his personal tragedy becoming a benefit for countless others then and for decades into the future. God often works like that. I am sorry for things I did in the past. But I mustn't regret them because some good for some unknown people may come from the errors of my ways. I, therefore, don't regret the past, and, furthermore, I don't wish to shut the door on it. I never will make those same mistakes again. How about you?

Sober day 169
Does a woman in jail wish to shut the door on her past?

Today's post is a follow-up to yesterday's: *"We will not regret the past nor wish to shut the door on it."* I know a woman in jail who is there because of a dark past. We palled around years ago when I was drinking and she was drugging and stealing. Some of the stealing was from me. I don't know what kept me following her around. Maybe it was because she was pretty and my marriage was crumbling apart.

Anyway, this week, she texted me for the first time in ages. She has life-threatening heart problems now. She wants to be friends again, presumably because her boyfriend and other friends, unlike me, got smart enough to desert her. She wants to change and remain sober. She wants me to be her life coach. I am flattered. Yet how does one trust someone who has violated his trust so many times before? Wait. Let me get back to my main point for this post. What about any regret for the past? Here was her text to me this afternoon:

> You have to find the positivity in the past, of how it made you stronger today. I believe I found life chasing death. I close the door, not on the past, but on the past demons that brought me down and put me in a dark place. But I find the positives of how they made me stronger today.

73

You can shut the door on the addiction and find positive reasons that it made you a stronger man today. Your struggles become strengths!

I don't think I can add anything meaningful to that.

Sober day 170
Is hearing me like listening to God?

Bill took my words right out of my mouth at AA. He expressed the way I feel when I share at meetings. As best as I can capture what he said, it went like this:

> I spent a lot of time sponsoring and making suggestions on sobering up, one-on-one. Then I felt led in a different direction. There was a time when I was convinced God wasn't with me, that he didn't care about me. That changed at an AA event when I could feel God inside me. I know God exists, and I know he is with me.

These days, I find myself moved to talk at meetings, more so than one-on-one conversations. That doesn't mean I turn my back on people who need help. It's just that God is leading me to something else. When I talk at AA meetings, like I'm doing now, I feel God putting the words in my mouth and guiding me to say something that someone there needs to hear. I say things that don't sound like me. *Where did that come from?* I know that it's God leading me to say what he wants me to say and what someone there needs to hear. I heard what Bill said and wrote his words here for you. I think God led him to say what he said so that I would listen and write them down. The message is for you and maybe for someone else who is reading this. Listen for God.

Sober day 179
Going up?

Everything happens for a reason. We hear it said often. Sometimes the reason becomes instantly apparent. Sometimes it never does. But God truly is working miracles, whether clear to us or not. Today's AA Daily Reflection is an example of God obviously working through someone and his fear, and it says:

> During the first three years of sobriety I had a fear of entering an elevator alone. One day I decided I must walk through this fear. I asked for God's help, entered the elevator, and there in the corner was a lady crying. She said that since her husband had died she was deathly afraid of elevators. I forgot my fear and comforted her. This spiritual experience helped me to see how willingness was the key to working the rest of the Twelve Steps to recovery. God helps those who help themselves.

Then there is the young woman I tried to help since childhood. She simply couldn't break her heroin addiction and she died last month. On the surface, it seemed she accomplished nothing and that her life was a waste of oxygen. But she left behind five children. I don't know what has happened to them now, but I expect one or more of those lives will someday make clear that their mother's life was not in vain.

Sober day 180
Every tool in the toolbox makes a difference

I tell people my ongoing recovery from alcoholism isn't attributed to one flash of light. Instead, I have a toolbox. A plethora of tools has led me here. There was AA, group therapy, a psychiatrist, medication, a therapist, my wife, books including the *Big*

Book, inpatient treatment, and more. It hasn't been one single tool. Following through with the metaphor of the toolbox, I heard a line at last night's AA meeting: "AA has a wrench to fit every nut." And speaking of nuts: "At AA, we're like a big bag of mixed nuts."

Sober day181
A time to write, a time to rest

We all get tired and run out of steam. Know what I mean? That's the way I am feeling about this literary gem I started. I ask myself, "Is God really guiding this endeavor?" Maybe. But he isn't exactly coaxing me along. I'm not feeling his guidance anymore. Is there any reward in all this? Yes, I'm out of steam like an old loco-motive. God, are you the engineer? This train seems to be going nowhere. I will blog again if and when I get back on track.

Sober day 362
Anybody out there?

I guess there is no one to say this to: I have been taking a blog-ging break. I am discouraged by the lack of readers, in spite of my efforts to publicize this thing. I felt like God asked me to blog when I started a year ago. Sadly, I sometimes wonder if God himself even reads my blog.

God, guide me to do your will.

Sober day 363
"First it ruins your life. Then it will take it"

I wrote yesterday I quit blogging due to a perceived lack of read-ership. That resulted in an avalanche of text messages (one, to be exact) pleading with me to continue. So I will. I found this letter in the advice column of the newspaper, and I thought it was worth sharing. Alcohol affects many more than just the alcoholic. See for yourself.

Dear Annie:

My wife is an alcoholic. I wrote the letter below to myself really. I was wondering if you would publish it, in hopes that it might help someone who is afflicted with alcoholism: I lost my wife and my best friend to alcoholism in March of 2012. That was seven long years ago. She continues to breathe, to function, to exist, but she is not the same person. Not even close. My wife used to light up a room with her laugh and her smile. Alcoholism has extinguished both. My world has not been the same since. As a husband, this disease makes me feel like an utter failure, haunted by 'maybes.' Maybe if I loved her a little more, the disease would go away. Maybe if I gave her a little more attention, she could beat this evil. Maybe if I was a little more patient, things would improve. To date, I have found it impossible to protect her from herself. Maybe that's not my job, but I feel as if I must try. Alcoholism is a cruel disease. It does not discriminate. It hits the wealthy and the poor. It can afflict Catholics, Jews, Protestants and Muslims. It affects men and women, young and old. Whites, blacks, Asians—it doesn't care. It first robs you of your judgment and senses, and then it goes to work on your character, your will. It will erode your self-esteem. Eventually, it will rob you of your soul and spirit. And in extreme cases, it will send you to an early grave. First, it ruins your life. Then, it will take it. While I believe in God, my prayers have gone unanswered to date. While us mere mortals lack the ability to understand how a just God could allow bad things to happen to good people, it is apparent God doesn't

work on our time. He works in his time. God
operates on a plane that is unrecognizable and
mysterious. My wish, my prayer, is that my wife
can somehow rid herself of this dreaded disease
before it's too late. She has a husband who feels
he has 'failed' to reach her, and three kids who
no longer recognize her, but whose collective love
continues unabated and unconditionally. The
collateral damage that this disease causes is enor-
mous, spreading like ripples in a lake. It affects
everyone around the individual who is suffering. Please, God, give my wife the courage and
strength to say: "No. Enough. I will no longer
succumb to alcoholism. I am bigger, better and
far more powerful than this disease ever dreamed
of. I am surrounded by people who love me and
depend on me, and I have a lot to live for."

—*Anonymous*

Sober day 366
One candle on my cake today

In the vernacular of Alcoholics Anonymous, every year of sobriety marks a birthday. It's a celebration of the day our new life began.
Today is my first birthday! Happy birthday to me! I made it through
the first year of sobriety by living, as they say in AA, "one day at a
time." AA participants mark birthdays in whatever way suits them.
In my case, my sponsor, Danny, called the AA offices in downtown
Louisville or somewhere to get my one-year token. At my home group
meeting, someone brought cupcakes, and the facilitator left a few
minutes at the end to recognize my achievement. I stood at the front
of the room with Danny after a hug while he spoke of my dedication
to stop drinking. My wife, Kathy, attended the meeting to show her
support and love for the new person I had become.

"I am grateful that I made it to my first birthday," I began. "I
want to thank my wife, Kathy, here for her support. She easily could

have left me, and she almost did. But she gave me a chance, and I am glad this time I haven't relapsed and let her down.

"Thank you, Danny, for always being there for me. You and AA have become an important part of my life. AA is one of three factors that have helped me stay sober. The second, as I mentioned, is my wife and family. We get sober and stay sober for ourselves only. But having a cheering section supporting me doesn't hurt.

"The third factor that helped me make it to my first birthday is God. That's the most important part. I pray every day and ask him to help me do his will. His will for me is to be a sober role model so that I can help others seek him and find him (AA Step 3: Made a decision to turn our will and our lives over to the care of God as we understood Him). Whether we are alcoholics or not, we need God in our lives. Thank you, God, for coming into mine. Thank you, all."

One more key to my sobriety is something I didn't mention at my birthday party but is something I want you readers to consider. At one of my group therapy sessions a while back, Chad mentioned he had started taking a prescription of Antabuse (disulfiram). A psychiatrist he was seeing prescribed it for him. It's a drug that makes one extremely sick if one drinks alcohol. So I made an appointment with his doctor, who prescribed Antabuse for me last April. I don't know if drinking really would make me violently ill, but I'm not taking any chances. I'm told that I could quit taking the drug for four or five days and then safely drink without puking. But I never plan to drink several days ahead of time. It has always been a sudden whim. Therefore, Antabuse is working for me. So that's what has kept me sober for an entire year: my wife and (two grown) kids, Danny and AA, my higher power, and Antabuse.

Sober day 367
How to take the best self challenge

I have been looking today to identify my best self and my toxic self. This comes from an episode of Dr. Phil yesterday. It strikes me as a different way of doing Step 4: "Made a searching and fearless moral inventory of ourselves."

Life Coach Mike Bayer was on the show. He told two mom/ sisters, "When you're your best self, you're being your authentic self, so our best authentic self. The anti-self is the characteristics that we think get in the way of being our best self."

In other words, what are the messages you tell yourself about you? He had them list their authentic selves, draw a picture of what that might look like, then give it a name. Then they did the same for their toxic selves. Watch the video.

Sober day 368
As we understood him

A lot of people I hear share at AA meetings struggled with the God concept. They didn't believe in a higher power and feared at the beginning that meant they were condemned to a life of drinking. That wasn't my issue. I believed in God. What I didn't believe in was the vengeful, punishing God of the Old Testament. I also had trouble believing the Christian doctrine I came from, which states no one gets into heaven unless they believe the same as they. They claim that a failure to follow New Testament preaching is a guarantee that your soul is headed for that bad hot place. The AA founders, in my opinion, had the right idea about spirituality. They didn't tell us what to believe. They simply said believe. Period. "Bill's Story" in the *Big Book* describes how that came about.

> *The word God still aroused a certain antipathy. When the thought was expressed that there might be a God personal to me this feeling was intensified. I didn't like the idea… I have since talked with scores of men who felt the same way. My friend suggested what then seemed a novel idea. He said, "Why don't you choose your own conception of God?" That statement hit me hard. It melted the icy intellectual mountain in whose shadow I had lived and shivered many years. I stood in the sunlight at*

last. "It was only a matter of being willing to believe in a power greater than myself. Nothing more was required of me to make my beginning."

We don't have to subscribe to stories about Sodom and Gomorrah turning into pillars of salt or loaves and fishes magically feeding thousands. Instead, we merely have to accept the existence of a higher power. It is that power I seek to serve. Thank you, AA founders, for straightening me out.

Sober day 369
Allow God to blow your mind

I wrote yesterday about accepting God as you understand him. What happens to us after we find God? It changes our lives in a good way. Read what it did for Bill W., the subject of yesterday's post:

> *I must turn all things to the Father of Light who presides over us all... The effect was electric. There was a sense of victory, followed by such a peace and serenity as I had never known. There was utter confidence. I felt lifted up, as though the great clean wind of a mountain top blew through and through.*

Wow! Overstated? Maybe a little, for some of us. But the difference in Bill W. was obvious.

> *For a moment, I was alarmed and called my friend, the doctor, to ask if I were still sane. "Something has happened to you I don't understand. But you had better hang on to it. Anything is better than the way you were." For if an alcoholic failed to perfect and enlarge his spiritual life through work and self-sacrifice for others, he could not survive the certain trials and low spots ahead.*

Sober day 371
I see God's masterpiece, a life in transition

This is a challenging post to write. If I tell the whole story, I will threaten the anonymity of an AA newcomer. But I'm going to try because the serendipity with which God works is blatantly obvious in what is happening in her life.

I was friends with a family twenty years ago. More precisely, I had a love and concern for the children who I saw growing up in a high-risk environment. I later watched from a distance with only occasional contact as the kids passed into adulthood, witnessing sad results of their troubled childhoods.

I never really knew one of the kids because she was just a baby back then, waddling through the house, wearing only a diaper or less. Later, I heard some heartbreaking, secondhand and thirdhand stories about her as she grew up. "*God, grant me the serenity to accept the things I cannot change.*" Sadly, she and her siblings were among those "things" I could not change.

Through Facebook, her father confided concerns for the now young woman. She came up on my Facebook list of friend suggestions, so I sent her a request, explaining who I was and how I knew who she was. The request was accepted, but that was all I heard back.

Months passed, and I thought of her little, except when her father told me his frustrations with her drug addiction and violent outbursts. Then, just after Christmas, I saw this posting from her on Facebook: "Who goes to NA or AA meetings? Need some people to go with! Just message me!"

I wrote back and offered her a ride to a meeting. Since then, we have become good friends. She lives in a halfway house, just a couple miles from me. I've been taking her to meetings almost every day. "*The courage to change the things I can.*"

She confided she has lived a drug-filled life. Her mother and friends provided her junk. She was sexually abused by many men ever since she was a little girl. Her own mother let her own boyfriend rape her over and over.

The girl has now been sober two months following homelessness, jail time, and hospitalization in a psych ward. Her mind is like that of a fourteen-year-old, socially and mentally frozen in time by drug abuse. But now, praise God, she seems committed to change. She asked me to be her life coach, and at AA yesterday, she found a sponsor, who I highly recommended to her.

God is at work in this woman. He brought us together because of my work with kids some twenty years ago. She lives close by me. He has led a sponsor into her life. My new friend has a lot of growing and learning to do, but I see God working miracles in her, in me too.

Sober day 372
"Vive la différence!"

As a child, I wondered why my Catholic cousins didn't see church and worship the same way my Presbyterian family did. I guess they must be wrong. After all, my parents told us we didn't need to kneel in church, that preachers preached in English, and that women didn't have to cover their heads in church. Later, I realized none of the differences mattered. We all worshipped the same higher power. We just did it differently.

If there are seventy thousand people at a college football game, how many of them saw the same game? Answer: none. Everyone saw each play a little bit differently. The game didn't look the same to those in end-zone seats as it did to those watching from the 50. Those in the luxury boxes didn't see the game the same way as those in the press box. Those cheering for the visiting team saw each play differently from the home fans in the row behind them. Certainly, the referees weren't watching the same game as everybody else was!

So why then should we expect everyone to see God in the same way? You have your perspective and I have mine. So what? Pray simply that God will help you do his will, not yours. And certainly not mine!

Sober day 373
Try writing about your favorite subject: yourself

I've been advised, as part of my recovery, to keep a daily journal. I guess that's what I've done with these passages you are reading. I hereby offer you the same words of wisdom I received. But instead of writing every day, try writing an autobiography. After all, you're the expert. No one knows your life any better than you do.

If you're not into writing, the thought of an autobiography might seem overwhelming. Remember that no one ever will see what you write, unless you decide to share it. Therefore, no one will be judging your work. You don't have to be a prince or princess of prose. Just write down whatever comes into your head. And if even *you* don't like what you wrote, then don't read it. It's the act of writing that is the therapy, not the verbiage.

One of the outpatient programs I attended passed out suggestions for writing an autobiography. They suggested beginning in your childhood (of course) with a specific focus on your drug or alcohol history.

1. How did it all begin?
2. Next, how have you attempted to control your alcohol use, including cutting down, changing friends, changing drugs, counseling, etc.?
3. List the kinds, amounts, and frequency of various chemicals, including alcoholic beverages, prescribed medications, over-the-counter meds, illegal drugs, and other mind-altering substances.
4. How has your drinking affected your health? Falls, traffic accidents, bar fights, organ damage?
5. What has drinking done to your emotional life?
6. How has drinking affected your leisure, recreational, and social life?
7. Has drinking affected your spiritual life or caused you to compromise your values?
8. How has it affected your family life?

9. What legal problems has your drinking led to?
10. What have been the financial ramifications of your drinking?
11. How has your use of drugs or alcohol affected your character (i.e., honesty, generosity, caring for others)?
12. What techniques have you tried to get your addiction under control? What has worked? If you aren't there yet, set aside your autobiography and add this chapter to it later.

Sober day 374
Ending one bad habit doesn't deserve another

Alcoholics have some sort of addictive tendency in their brains. Giving up alcohol dependency is all well and good, unless it is replaced with some other kind of dependency, physical and/or psychological. Those who build their recovery around being free from all mind-altering drugs have by far the best chance to avoid relapse.

The first group therapy program I tried was with the Jefferson Alcohol and Drug Abuse Center (JADAC) in Louisville, Kentucky. There I received a surprising list of medications to avoid. The warning was that I might switch my addiction to any of these chemicals. Here is a list of drugs that could be hazardous to my health and yours. Save it for future reference.

- All sedatives, hypnotics, including barbiturates such as Nembutal, Seconal, Tuinal, Phenobarbital, Ambien, Lunesta, Sonata, Doriden, Quaalude, Dalmane, and Placidyl.
- All narcotics and pain-relieving medications including opiates such as morphine, heroin, and codeine. Likewise, synthetic narcotics such as Dilaudid, Demerol, Darvon, Talwin, Percodan, Percocet, Darvocet, Lortabs, Oxycodone, Oxycontin, Methadone, Ultram, and Ultracet.
- All tranquilizers, including Meprobamate, Miltown, Equanil, Librium, Xanax, Valium, Klonopin, and any benzodiazepine.

- No Requip or Lyrica.
- All antihistamines such as Ephedrine, Pseudo-Ephedrine, or Sudafed.
- Over-the-counter medications containing antihistamines and scopolamine, such as Nytol, Sominex, Contact, Dristan, etc.
- Muscle relaxants such as Flexeril, Soma, Baclofen, Skelaxin, Robaxin, etc.
- Even energy drinks such as those produced by Mtn Dew, Amp, Red Bull, and SoBe.
- Cough medicines containing narcotics, alcohol, antihistamines.
- Weight-control tablets such as Mini-thins (white crosses, etc.).
- Reserpine compounds, which are basically tranquilizers or preparations containing reserpine prescribed for hypertension, should be used with caution and only when absolutely necessary.
- Products meant to keep you alert such as NoDoz and Ephedra.
- Alcoholic beverages, including nonalcoholic beer or near beer.
- Stimulants, including amphetamines (Dexedrine, Benzedrine, etc.), Ritalin.
- Marijuana and other "street drugs," including Special K, Ecstasy, crystal meth, cocaine, crack, etc.

Sober day 375
And now a word about codependency

I haven't written anything about codependency yet, even though there's often a relationship between addicts and codependents. Looking back, I don't see that my wife suffered from codependency. I'll have to ask her for her thoughts. Codependents can include spouses, children, parents, grandchildren, siblings, and others. Anyone living in a family of denial, compulsive behavior, and emotional repression is vulnerable to codependence, even if there is no alcoholism or chemical dependency in the family. Codependency is an unhealthy way of relating to others, with low self-esteem at the heart of it. Codependents suffer from a progression of focusing attention on someone else and neglecting their own feelings and needs.

Not to confuse you, but I'm going to share with you three clinical definitions of codependency. See if you or someone close to you can relate. Tomorrow I'll list some of the symptoms of codependency.

Codependency is "an emotional, psychological, and behavioral condition that develops as a result of an individual's prolonged exposure to...a set of oppressive rules—rules which prevent the open expression of feeling" (Robert Subby, director of Family Systems, Inc., Minneapolis).

Codependency is "a term used to describe an exaggerated dependent pattern of learned behaviors, beliefs, and feelings that make life painful. It is a dependence on people and things outside the self to the point of having little self-identity" (Sondra Smalley, director of Dependencies Institute of Minnesota).

Codependency is "a specific condition that is characterized by preoccupation and extreme dependence (emotionally, socially, and sometimes physically) on a person or object. Eventually, this dependence on another person becomes a pathological condition that affects the co-dependent in all other relationships" (Sharon Wegscheider-Cruse, president of Onsite Training and Consulting, Inc., Sioux Falls).

Sober day 376
How to recognize codependency

As a follow-up to yesterday's blog, I found lots of symptoms of codependency online. Here is one I like.

1. You're overly concerned about what the other person is doing, thinking, and feeling—and you want to fix or rescue them from their problems.

You worry that if you don't take care of them, something bad will happen.

2. Your relationship is consistently one-sided; one person is hardworking and responsible and the other is allowed to be irresponsible or avoid the consequences of their actions. You may enable and make excuses for the other person's poor choices.

3. You sacrifice yourself to make the other person happy. This can include your health, time, energy, money, values, goals, or friendships. Your life revolves around the other person—making them happy, taking care of them, doing what they want to do.

4. You 'walk on eggshells' around the other person, afraid of doing or saying something that will displease or anger them. As a result, you may not express your opinions, share your feelings, or ask for what you want. And, to avoid conflict, you may say yes to things that you don't want to do or that don't align with your values or goals.

5. You act like a martyr, taking care of everyone and everything, but resentful that no one helps or seems to care for you.

6. Your need to fix or rescue becomes controlling. You attempt to control the other person's behavior through criticism, ultimatums, nagging, or giving unsolicited advice.

7. You continue the relationship even after the other person has repeatedly hurt you (physically, emotionally, financially, etc.).

8. You spend more time taking care of others than taking care of yourself. And when you do something for yourself, like rest, enjoy a hobby, or practice self-care, you feel guilty or selfish.

9. You're afraid of being rejected, criticized, or abandoned.
10. You often feel resentful, frustrated, taken advantage of, or unfulfilled.

Sober day 377
How to break out of unhealthy codependent behaviors

There are lots of causes of codependency as I've tried to relate in the past two days. One of those is to live with or be close to an alcoholic. Read yesterday to determine whether you may be codependent. Read below to determine how to get out of a codependent relationship. Being codependent does neither you nor the alcoholic any good.

Increase your self-worth. Often, codependents feel like there's something wrong with them, so they constantly seek validation, are afraid of rejection, and do things to prove their worth. They become caretakers and need to be needed. Instead of focusing solely on what others need, we can start considering our own needs. We can acknowledge and validate our own feelings and treat ourselves with compassion. These things aren't easy to do, but we can take small, intentional actions toward this goal such as saying something kind to ourselves or setting a boundary.

Get to know yourself better. As codependents, we get so wrapped up in people-pleasing and taking care of others, that we often become disconnected from ourselves. You may no longer know what you feel or think because you've suppressed them for so long or you may not pursue your goals or hobbies because you gave them up to spend your time and energy doing what others are interested in.

So you may need to get reacquainted with yourself. You can begin by asking yourself: What do I like to do? Who do I want to spend time with? What are my goals? What can I do for myself to feel better? I encourage you to pick one thing that you can do for yourself and start today. Putting yourself on your to-do list is an important part of bringing your life back into balance and health.

Let go—just a little. The concept of detaching is central to codependency recovery. When you detach, you put some emotional or physical space between yourself and others. It doesn't mean abandoning others or ending relationships. And it's not selfish or unloving. Detaching means you stop obsessing about what others are doing or not doing, their problems, feelings, and so forth. It gives you room to be yourself and take care of yourself. Detaching includes:

- not engaging in arguments;
- leaving a situation that's uncomfortable or unsafe;
- staying calm rather than reacting;
- considering your own feelings and needs;
- choosing not to enable unhealthy or dangerous behaviors;
- listening rather than trying to solve or fix problems;
- not nagging and criticizing; and
- setting boundaries.

Get emotional support. Relationships are hard, especially when they aren't going well. Emotional support can help reduce feelings of loneliness and shame and increase motivation and accountability. A therapist can be a useful sounding board and help you better understand and change yourself. You don't have to do it alone.

Thanks to *Psychology Today* for this information.

Sober day 381
A weekly steeplechase should be a never-ending marathon

I went to church last Sunday. A woman from a halfway house who designated me as her life coach (I wrote about her on Sober Day 371) wanted me to go with her and her father. I don't know if I will go again this week. Maybe if I am invited. Definitely not if I'm not asked.

It's a Baptist church, very well attended last week. Sure, people were nice. But only three welcomed me and introduced themselves. Of course, I didn't approach them. I was a stranger playing on their home field.

AA people are friendlier. Maybe because it's not a clique. Maybe because we know we automatically have something in common. We all are there for the same reason.

Correct me if I am wrong, but church people are church people for various reasons. Some are there to praise and thank God. Some are there for the music, some for the sermon. Others want to socialize. Some want to be seen. Some seek forgiveness, some give gratitude to the Lord. There are those who don't give God much thought until same time next week.

Alcoholics need constant reinforcement from others and never-ending love from God. I speak for many when I say AA is a spiritual booster shot whenever needed. All are there for one reason: a desire to stop drinking. If an AA member forgets God till next week, there may be trouble ahead. God got us out of our mess, and he keeps us out of it every day we pray to him and know he cares about us.

Sober day 706
A new format, but the messages remain relevant (I hope)

I stopped writing this blog because upon checking the stats regularly, I had zero visitors most of the time. To continue blogging would be for my own therapy and no one else's. I want to share what I have learned about life and abstinence along my journey to a lasting sobriety. Maybe some nugget will help someone else—if they read it. So I decided to turn my musings into a book. I felt, from the start, God wanted me to write this blog. Now I feel he is leading me in a slightly different direction. Whether you are ingesting this message via blog or book, I invite you to eat it all up, meditating on the messages that apply to you and passing up what doesn't. Somewhere in these words, I hope that God is leading you to a place where you need to be led. That's what he did for me.

Sober day 707
Sobriety in a time of crisis

Are you staying sober during the pandemic? Here is a Dr. Phil interview with a woman who started drinking every day to stay "comfortably numb." Have a look. It lasts less than five minutes.

The QR code on the right is the conclusion to the above. The woman confesses she is self-medicating.

I don't want to be like her. So far, I am as sober as a nun.

Sober day 712
Coronavirus brings unique risks to recovering alcoholics

Comments at the AA meeting I attended Thursday night got me to thinking about the coronavirus and how it might be particularly hazardous to us alcoholics. For example, I used to be an impulse drinker. Even though I was trying to stop, I could find excuses to buy another bottle. The coronavirus seems like a good excuse to people who may be like I was. "What the heck. So what if I get sick? I might be quarantined. I might choose to isolate myself and stay home away from people. Guess I might as well stock up with whiskey and drink my way through the pandemic."

My Thursday meeting was poorly attended. It might have been because of the storms around us at the same time. Maybe people were social distancing to the max. What I do know is that a week ago, we had more at that meeting than ever before. I hear many alcoholics say they *have* to go to AA to stay well-grounded and sober.

So what will happen to these people if most others stop going? And what if churches where some meetings are held, including my Thursday night meeting, lock their doors to AA? After all, the Kentucky governor has strongly suggested churches discontinue services and programs.

AA meetings across town, across the state, and across the world are vulnerable to cancellation and weak attendance. If you are a recovering alcoholic susceptible to these scenarios, be sure you have something else in your bag of tricks to ensure you don't allow the coronavirus to cause a relapse. For me, AA isn't my only savior from the demon rum. I can rely on other booze repellants.

Speaking of Savior, remember that God is still with you. This is a test of our spirituality and sobriety. Don't let John Barleycorn lead you down the wrong highway. Stay strong, pray, and call others, such as your sponsor. These extraordinary times are no excuse to let your sobriety slip away.

Sober day 718
Bridge over the River Cry

Some of the bridges I burned were the wrong ones. Others I should have crossed, but I sat at the side of the road, too often drinking. Now I'm sober. I feel God with me. I pray to do his will. Now he leads me across the right bridges and gives me lighter fluid to torch the bridges I need to burn.

Sober day 719
This goalie allowed too many "shots" to get past him

I'm an unapologetic hockey fan. I remember when my beloved Pittsburgh Penguins won their second consecutive Stanley Cup, and Ed Belfour was the goalie for the Chicago Blackhawks. He's a Hall of Famer now. But in the decisive game, he got pulled because the Penguins were getting everything they shot past him. Move forward nineteen years. Here's what happened to "Eddie the Eagle." He was arrested in Bowling Green, Kentucky, on January 28, facing one count of third-degree criminal mischief and one count of public intoxication. He paid $219 in fines and court costs.

Man, I wish I had gotten off that easy. Here's more of the story.

Police responded to a complaint of "a drunk and disorderly person" at a hotel, where they found Belfour lying on the floor of the hotel's second level by the spa room. "Belfour was clutching a curtain rod that had been ripped out of the drywall above a window next to him," according to the citation, which also noted that he had "slurred speech, bloodshot eyes, he could barely stand up, and he had the strong odor of alcohol on his breath."

The 911 caller told police Belfour was drinking downstairs, tried to fight a hotel employee, and struck a glass window before staggering upstairs and trying to force his way into the spa room. The 911 caller was locked inside.

During and after his career, Belfour faced legal trouble with several arrests involving alcohol. He retired from hockey in 2007.

Do you suppose Eddie is now on the narrow path to sobriety? Well, maybe. But he is the president and CEO of Belfour Spirits, a whiskey company he started with family members. How convenient!

Sober day 721
Souper tips for the recovering alcoholic

As I write this, the spread of the coronavirus is the big story around the world. For those with symptoms, here is some chicken soup—*Chicken Soup for the Soul*, that is. I bought it for a couple bucks at a Goodwill store and finished reading it this morning.

The last item is "100 Gifts to Give All Year Long." I will pull out a few items that I think are valuable for us alcoholics:

- Smile.
- Provide a shoulder to lean on.
- Pat someone on the back.
- Ignore a rude remark.
- Pay your bills on time.
- Give your used clothes to a needy person.

- Say something nice to someone.
- Catch someone doing it right and say, "Great job!"
- Tell the truth but with kindness and tact. Ask, "Does the other person really need to hear this?" (Fits with AA Step 9).
- Do a kind deed anonymously.
- Listen.
- Lighten up. Find the funny side of a situation.
- Take a quiet walk when you feel like blowing your top.
- Look for something beautiful in one person every day.
- Ask a friend for help, even when you don't need it.
- Point out the beauty and wonder of nature to those you love.
- Allow someone a mistake.
- Allow yourself several mistakes.
- Let go of the urge to be critical of someone.

Sober day 722
Join online AA meetings to avoid coronavirus

I hesitated about going to my usual Thursday night AA group. I'm glad I went because I found something better. I was reminded about online AA meetings. I may have blogged about them before, but if so, I forget. This sounded like a good alternative to being exposed to possible coronavirus carriers. Plus, next week, I am having knee replacement surgery and won't be able to drive for a month or two. Online meetings sound like a good option for someone homebound like me.

Check it out at. This could be a valuable tool in your recovery process, especially during these unusual times.

Sober day 723
How to eavesdrop on AA-like online group meetings

I stumbled across a series of podcasts today by the McShin Recovery Foundation, which is posting recovery meetings online. The meetings are intended to reinforce sobriety against a backdrop of coronavirus and quarantines.

A good place to start is news coverage of the nonprofit's online groups, namely Channel 6 in Richmond, Virginia.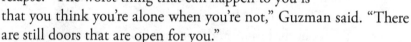

During coronavirus, self-quarantining may be the best defense against the pandemic. But Nellie Guzman, who battled drug and alcohol addiction for five years, said isolation can be a recipe for relapse. "The worst thing that can happen to you is that you think you're alone when you're not," Guzman said. "There are still doors that are open for you."

According to another participant, "An idle mind is a devil's mind. Boredom is a big trigger for us addicts… Watch what is online. Definitely. If you can't get out, watch the groups online. Call another addict. You got to want it. You got to chase that recovery."

McShin Foundation cofounder John Shinholser said peer-to-peer recovery is paramount in overcoming addiction. "A lot of people across America can't get to their meetings or groups, so we're doing a big push on social media so people at home can feel like a part of a group and part of recovery."

These groups are well-worth investigating.

Sober day 725
Why I quit AA

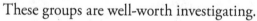

I haven't let the pandemic keep me away from AA—until now. Signs on the door at my home group meetings warned that masks are required, stay six feet away from others, and limit meetings to fifteen people. That worked for a while. But lately, more chairs are being added to the room to give space to more than fifteen people. Some aren't wearing masks or aren't wearing them correctly over their noses.

The news says close to three thousand people are dying of coronavirus every day across the country. That's how many died on 9/11! Closer to home, Louisville reports more than twenty deaths every day. That's why I won't go to AA anymore. We need to get the coronavirus under control. The president isn't helping. The Kentucky governor is trying. I feel like I need to do my part to protect myself and my family. I'm staying home. Self-isolation. Stay well, my readers.

Sober day 726
Thy rod and thy staph don't comfort me.

Woe is me. I'm having a bad day.

I was scheduled to have knee replacement surgery this week, but I was diagnosed with a staph infection on my hip. I don't know where that came from, but it means my surgery is postponed. Some days, my knee isn't too bad. But on others, like today, it's hard to walk. Furthermore, I decided to stop going to AA meetings so I won't catch or pass the coronavirus. See yesterday. I texted my sponsor a moment ago to alert him that I don't plan to attend meetings for a while. I promised to call if I get a craving to drink.

I don't expect that to happen. I haven't been tempted since my sobriety date last May. AA helps with that. Writing this blog helps. God helps me even more. I pray often to do his will through me. I'm fairly certain his will isn't for me to relapse.

I am more-or-less homebound for now because it hurts to walk and I don't want to catch the coronavirus.

Sober day 727
It was the best of reasons, the worst of reasons

I am taking advantage of staying put so I don't participate in catching and spreading the coronavirus. I'm watching a lot of TV shows I've recorded. This afternoon, it's the 1935 version of *A Tale of Two Cities*. After being acquitted for treason, Charles Darnay dines with his defense lawyer, a drunk named Sydney Carton, and asks him why drink so much. Carton says, "You are smug, Mr. Darnay, to ask why people drink, but I will tell you. So that they can stand their fellow men better. And after a few bottles, I might even like you."

I can identify. I got along just fine with others during and after drinking. Some drunks are fighters, some are lovers. I clearly was the latter.

Now, sober, I find God to be a much better catalyst to tolerate my fellow men. God wants us to love everyone, even those hard to love. Since I seek to do God's will, I now find it easy to care about others; maybe even "stand (my) fellow men better."

Sober day 728
He restoreth my soul

God led me to AA, and then AA led me to God.

Sober day 729
COVID-19 test? I'll drink to that!

I am doing my part to halt the spread of the coronavirus. I wash my hands and use hand sanitizer. I wear a mask in public. I leave my house only when I have a real need. And this morning, I had a COVID-19 test.

It's no longer necessary to display symptoms to get a test. Kentucky Governor, Steve Beshear, during his daily news briefings, encourages all to take a test. I made an appointment online. There was no waiting. I drove up, cracked my window, and received a swab and a vial. Sticking that baby up my nose made me sneeze like crazy. That was the only discomfort. For my effort, I received a mask, tissues, and a bottle of hand sanitizer. No charge. The hand sanitizer has the consistency of water—or whiskey—not like lotion. According to the label, it consists of 80 percent alcohol. Eighty percent? Do you know what I would have been tempted to try to do with that if I were still drinking and was out of booze? Yuk! But if I could drink a bottle of mouthwash back in my crazy days, I probably, might have, maybe tried a sip, then more.

Well, didn't our beloved president wonder on live TV if he could ingest antiseptic to cure or prevent the coronavirus? Don't get me started on him.

Sober day 730
Why I don't jog to the liquor store anymore

Running long distances was once my passion. I ran races anywhere from 6.2 miles to 50 miles. Compared to other runners, I was okay but certainly not a standout. What mattered was competing against myself by reducing my times. The bottom line was keeping fit and healthy and, unlike my father, living to be older than forty-nine.

I was maybe in my prime when my knee started bothering me. I ran through it. *Don't let a little bit of pain slow me down*, I thought. *Rub some dirt on it and sign up for another race. Ignore the problem, and it will go away.*

It didn't work out that way. I eventually had to see a doctor. After arthroscopic surgery and a long recovery, I went back to running. My knee still hurt and kept getting worse. I ignored the problem. It still didn't go away. "Problems do not go away. They must be worked through or else they remain, forever a barrier to the growth and development of the spirit," wrote M. Scott Peck in *The Road Less Traveled*.

My inability to run without pain was one factor among others that led me to depression and a belief that drinking would make the physical and emotional pain go away. Alcohol led to more alcohol, which led to alcoholism. My knee still hurt. Sometimes, I ran in my neighborhood while kind of drunk.

Dr. Peck says: "We ignore (problems), forget them, pretend they do not exist. We even take drugs to assist us in ignoring them, so that by deadening ourselves to the pain we can forget the problems that cause the pain."

I still can't run. I will have knee replacement surgery after the coronavirus pandemic is under some control. Meanwhile, I work out using an elliptical machine and a treadmill in my basement, and I walk when the weather is good. Most important, I don't drink anymore. Any and all exercises are better for me than bending my elbow to raise booze to my lips.

Sober day 731
Year 2: Another one bites the dust

Today, I blow out two candles on my sobriety birthday cake. I hear people say how difficult it is to make it this far after years of drinking. For some people, I'm sure it is. But for me, sobriety brings me joy. I feel God's presence every day as I try to understand and then do his will. Quitting was the hard part. "Staying quit" has been much easier for me. The temptation always will be there for me. Remember that the disease is called alcoholism, not "alcoholwasm." I had far fewer years of abusing alcohol than many of the people I hear from at AA meetings. Many started drinking and drugging as teenagers, and as the years rolled by, their abuse became worse. And then worse. I was well into my fifties before a few sips turned into a few gulps.

Then, for years, I didn't want to stop, even though drinking was bringing me severe consequences. It wasn't until I wanted to quit drinking badly enough that I tried prescription Antabuse. I heard about it from a fellow member of group therapy. Taking that medication supposedly leads to violent sickness, if one drinks while taking it. I never tried to see if it really works. I mean, I drank for a lot of reasons, but violent illness was never one of them. All that matters is I wanted to stop drinking badly enough that I drove all over the county looking for Antabuse after my usual pharmacy apparently didn't stock it anymore.

Now two whole years! It makes me wonder why it took me so long to stop because my life is so much better now. If you are ready to stop drinking, seek a psychiatrist (if you don't see one already) who can write you a prescription for Antabuse. Then, if you want to test the sickness side effect that comes from drinking, let me know how that goes for you. As for me, it's been a wonderful two years.

Sober day 732
Drinking doesn't selectively numb

I drank to numb myself from hurts and negative feelings. In doing so, I have come to find out I also numbed my feelings of joy, happiness, creativity, love—all my positive emotions. We need to accept our pains so that we don't numb ourselves to God and the glory of living.

> We cannot *selectively numb* emotions. When we *numb* the painful emotions, we also *numb* the positive emotions. Vulnerability sounds like truth and feels like courage. Truth and courage aren't always comfortable, but they're never weakness. (Brené Brown)

Sober day 735
The need for face-to-face contact to stay sober

Dr. Phil talks to a woman nearly four years sober who understands the need we have to be around others. Note that she worked the 12 Steps. The video is short and worth a listen:

Sober day 736
"Isolation has been very boring"

Speaking of Dr. Phil, it doesn't matter if you like him or his show. Take a listen to this woman who is ten months sober, living in a treatment facility, and trying to maintain her sobriety. Here is her brief interview with Dr. Phil:

Sober day 739
Permit yourself to fear snarling dogs and pandemics

Rumination may be fine for cows, but it's an unhealthy human response to stress. Rumination of the people kind is an inability to let go of something, which can lead to depression, which can lead to withdrawal from other people. For more, listen to Dr. Ramani Durvasula.

She goes on to say that normal anxiety is a fear of something that is real. Being afraid of snarling dogs is not anxiety, it's a normal response. Likewise, being anxious during a pandemic is normal. Don't sweat it, accept it. Ask God to help you control the feelings you can control and give you the serenity to accept those things you have absolutely no control over. Feeling in control can mean avoiding the temptation to self-medicate with alcohol. If you are anxious about getting sick, about your elderly parents getting sick, about the loss of a job, about a dried-up bank account—these feelings are normal. No one, including you, is to blame.

A video by Dr. Tracey Marks offers five practical ways to manage coronavirus anxiety:

1. Focus on what you *can* control.
2. Find creative ways to virtually connect with people.
3. Keep a structured day, even if you are not working.
4. Limit your time watching the news.
5. Spend more time outside getting fresh air.

Sober day 740
God bless the brave, the compassionate, the exhausted

I need to digress today from my usual theme of sobriety and seeking a higher power. Instead, I will share a passage from *The Endless Practice* by Mark Nepo.

I don't know exactly what he was trying to say, but he hit a bull's-eye in today's battle against coronavirus. This passage is dedicated to doctors, nurses, paramedics, firefighters, and others who are on the front line, battling COVID-19, and it says:

> That we go numb along the way is to be expected. Even the bravest among us who give their lives to care for others, go numb with fatigue when the heart can take in no more, when we need time to digest all we meet. Overloaded and overwhelmed, we start to pull back from the world, so we can internalize what the world keeps giving us. Perhaps the noblest private act is the unheralded effort to return: to open our hearts once they have closed, to open our souls once they have shied away, to soften our minds once they've been hardened by the storms of our day...
> Our compassion waits there to revive us.

Sober day 742
Write your fear a letter from love

"There's nothing wrong with being afraid. Face fear, find love," says Elizabeth Gilbert.

Sober day 743
AA serves as my church away from church

Alcoholics Anonymous is like a church, only freer. Freer? More free sounds better. Either way, I've come to see many similarities between AA and church congregations but with important differences too.

In AA, people come from different economic status, different races, different life stories, different backgrounds. Churches are like that too, but, sadly, some churches don't display the diversity of AA. Both are (or think they are) cordial and welcoming. Members attend or should attend with a singleness of purpose: sobriety for one, worship for the other. Both preach helping others. It's a higher power that glues each group together. But AA and churches have some differences, for sure. AA has no structure, no hierarchical leadership, no paid positions. If AA were to tighten its ropes, it would lose the casual feel that cries, "Keep coming back!"

Churches have a way of complicating things. AA tells us to love God and people, act justly, love mercy, walk humbly, treat people as you want to be treated. If you want to be great, be a servant. Hey, you, AA-ers, doesn't that describe us well? Actually, these words come from Jen Hatmaker in *For the Love: Fighting for Grace in a World of Impossible Standards* as she describes what a church should be like. AA and churches, you see, seek to fill the same basic needs. Hatmaker goes on to describe churchgoers in a way I would describe AA members:

> It lets anyone in the door! All sorts of hooligans fill the sanctuaries: kind and good ones, angry and cynical ones, mean and judgmental ones, smart and funny ones, broken and sad ones, weird and awkward ones, precious and loving ones, scared and wounded ones, brave and passionate ones, insiders and outliers, newbies and lifers and trying-one-more-timers. Just a whole bunch of human people.

Yep. That sounds a lot like the AA meetings I attend.

Sober day 748
How to control stress and "healthify" your brain

Whether you're a fan of Dr. Phil or not (I am, but he annoys me sometimes), he comes up with good stuff and hosts some knowledgeable experts. That's true as he helps viewers deal with coronavirus from his kitchen at home.

Yesterday, he interviewed psychiatrist Dr. Daniel Amen (never forget that name. Let me hear you say "Amen!"). He claims some anxiety is good for you because it leads you to take proper safety measures. The students on spring break flooded the beaches and ignored the corona threat by not distancing themselves from others. They weren't anxious about the illness. Then they carried COVID-19 back north to their grandparents and others.

So a little anxiety, which may lead to stress, can protect us. However, chronic stress damages the hippocampus part of the brain, which controls memory and mood. Sleep—seven and a half to eight hours a night—and exercise restore the hippocampus cells. So does proper nutrition. Amen mentioned onions, mushrooms, and garlic in particular (don't forget your breath mints!). He adds that writing down negative thoughts helps us deal with them realistically. Guess what? Drinking alcohol doesn't restore your brain at all and even causes more damage. We all know that.

I heard someone at an AA meeting say drinking leads to the prison yard, the graveyard, or if we are fortunate, God's yard. Don't give in to the temptation to drink away your stress. It may help for a little while, but drinking adds to the stress—the bad kind of stress—as you return to sobriety.

I encourage you to watch Dr. Phil's interview with Dr. Amen. He offers great insights that I don't have room to share in this blog.

Sober day 749
"Be grateful for every little thing that makes you smile"

My friend Woody directed me to this message in Facebook. It applies to struggling alcoholics, quarantined pandemic victims, lonely shut-ins, and all people, all the time. Don't lose sight of the wonderful gifts God gives us every day.

Usually, most of us forget that every challenge that life gives us is a valuable lesson. No matter how hard it all gets, we should never forget to be grateful for what we have and who we are... There are people around us who love and support us unconditionally. We have a family that stands by us from the very beginning of our lives. What's more, we have friends who will always be there for us, no matter what. All of these loving human beings around us are the greatest treasure we can ask for. They give us strength, they give us love, they give us reasons to be alive. We should be grateful for each and every one of them.

We have a roof above our heads, we have food on the table, we see the sun every morning, and the moon every evening. These little things are what really matters in life. If we are not thankful for them, we wouldn't be able to see the beauty in anything else.

Along with all these significant little things we should be thankful for come our mistakes and flaws. After all, they are what make us human beings. Nothing in the world is perfect, and we make no exception.

Our mistakes are what builds our characters and turns us into the genuine people we are today...

For more, see:

Sober day 755
Now is the time for hope and strength

Coronavirus doesn't exist. Think positively. If there *is* a coronavirus, it will go away without affecting me, my family, or my friends. That's what I call "positive thinking." In reality, that's what I call hogwash. It is dangerous thinking. Wait. I do believe in positive thinking. But what exists in my "Pleasantville" doesn't exist in Louisville. People get sick. Divorce happens. Domestic violence is rampant. The police shot and killed someone's brother, son, and maybe father downtown, yesterday, because he pulled a weapon on police.

Bad stuff like COVID-19 exists. So do rainbows and butterflies. God gets us through the bad stuff and enables us to enjoy the good stuff. He tests us in many ways. My alcoholism was a test. It wasn't God's will, but he used my addiction to make me a better person, once I emerged from the darkness of the disease. Have faith in a higher power, and this too will pass. I opened up a book I read sometime back and came across a passage that supports what I'm trying to say. The book is *Awakening in Time* by Jacqueline Small. I've quoted her before. Please note what it says:

> True positive thinking means focusing in
> the direction of what is life-giving even while
> someone or something is in the process of being
> negative or even dying. It is about being willing
> to face every new moment, every new circum-

stance as it unfolds, with the hope and strength to deal with all that is occurring—both the terror and the bliss of transformation. In Twelve Step work, this is known as taking it "one day at a time"—and even one moment at a time.

How are you dealing with the coronavirus? We need the serenity to accept what we cannot change and the willingness to face everything with the hope and strength to deal with it all.

Sober day 756
"God could and would if he were sought"

We all know alcoholics who have gotten well. I hope you are one. I am one. At least, so far today, I am. Several years ago, I spent twenty-eight days at a residential treatment program. One of our facilitators claimed that 95 percent of us would return to drinking. I scoffed. Not me. But I did. Then I discovered a new way of life and a new way to see myself and my environment. Praise God for that! AA meetings put me in touch with other alcoholics on the road to recovery. One of those joyful travelers asked why some people get well and others don't. We decided the answer lies in a phrase from the *Big Book* that is part of every premeeting ritual: "God could and would if He were sought."

I used to think God chose me to get well because he has important things for me to do. But in reality, *I* chose me to recover. He does have important things for me to do, but I had to pick myself out of the gutter first. The keywords from the *Big Book* quote are "*if He were sought.*" We must take action if God is going to cure us from this fatal disease. I am sober because I want to be and I took a variety of measures to get there and stay there. God wants me to be sober and do his will. But if I were out there, still drinking, God would stand by as I threw myself on the junk pile of damaged souls. It's my choice and yours.

Sober day 757
Lead me not into temptation

A week after I left The Brook, the residential treatment program for addicts I mentioned yesterday, I attended my nephew's wedding outdoors. It was an ideal day for it. Nearby was a tent covering tables, a buffet, and a well-stocked bar. The open bar didn't bother me. I wasn't tempted to sneak a drink, although I probably would have tried if I weren't fresh off an intensive program.

I suppose you have found yourself in a similar situation if you are trying to stay sober. If not, you might wonder how strong your aversion is to the demon rum spread out before you. It's certain to happen sometime. It can go either way, depending on your resolve. Some need to avoid restaurants with bars and beer-swilling buddies. Others aren't tempted—for now, at least.

Someone at AA recently compared it to going to a barbershop: If you go to one, you will probably sooner or later get a haircut. So if you want long hair, I guess you better avoid places with razors and scissors.

Sober day 761
We're not addicts, we're HBWSSMPTTDKHTEFIETTPBs

Attention deficit disorder (ADD) is a result of trauma. That's the premise of Dr. Gabor Maté. Today, I want to shepherd you all to his YouTube piece on addiction. It's insightful and interesting. On the downside, it lasts an hour. I listened while I worked out on my exercise bike. Maybe you can simply prop up your feet and listen. Taking your PC outdoors on a pleasant day (as today is here) seems appealing. However you choose, you will find it worthwhile. He covers a variety of topics related to the psychology of addiction and the impacts of trauma on our lives. That's the reason for the lead sentence above. Take a listen. A wish he expressed was to have everyone who ever uses the word *addict* to instead say, "A human being who suffered so much pain that they didn't know how to escape from it except through this particular behavior."

That would change the conversation. It also would be very accurate. Great, but the acronym would be too long: HBWSSMPTTDKHTEFIETTPB. I'll stick to calling us addicts.

Sober day 762
Addicts believe the next time will be better than now

According to Dr. Gabor Maté in his book, *In the Realm of Hungry Ghosts*, "The addict dreads and abhors the present moment. They bend feverishly only toward the next time, the moment when the brain, infused with the drug of choice, will briefly experience itself as liberated."

I can identify with that. I won't say I abhorred the present moment, but I sure wasn't living in it. My enemy was "now," my hope was to somehow return to the past and start over. But that was impossible, so I tried to make my hurt go away by drinking. Clearly that just made me more miserable. The downward spiral continued until I was able to find the real me again. I'm grateful to God that the real me is much better than the old me or the drunk me. I am learning about myself and others in my new world of sobriety.

Sober day 763
Wanting a sandwich without works is hunger

"What does it profit, my brethren, if someone says he has faith but does not have works? Can faith save him? You believe that there is one God... But do you want to know, O foolish man, that *faith, without works, is dead*?" (James 2:14, 19–20 NKJV).

I wanted a sandwich for lunch today. I prayed for it, and because I feel like I have a close relationship with God, I had faith he would deliver me my sandwich. But no matter how much faith I have, God is no Jimmy John's. I had to rise from my chair, find my keys and wallet, and drive to the store. I told the man at the counter what I wanted, and he gave it to me. I had faith that he would, and he did. But I had to take action to get that sandwich. Yes, someone would have delivered it, but that would have taken a phone call. Again, faith, without the work, doesn't put lunch in my belly.

Are you praying for sobriety? Keep praying as you walk past the liquor store. Praying alone without action—without attending AA meetings, without a relationship with a higher power, without a sponsor, without helping others, without changing routines that led to drinking—makes avoiding those liquor shelves unlikely.

> *Now we need more action, without which we find that Faith without works is dead.* (AA *Big Book*, page 76)

Sober day 765
The easier, softer way is God

> *We thought we could find an easier, softer way. But we could not.* (The *Big Book*, page 58)

I didn't want to go to AA meetings or work steps or turn my will and my life over to the care of God. There must be an easier way, somehow, to control my drinking. Anyway, I didn't want to stop. Not completely. I tried limiting my drinking only to weekends. That didn't work. I tried limiting my drinking only to weekdays. That didn't work either. I tried drinking only late at night, after my wife went to bed. I tried drinking only in the mornings, when my wife was at work so that I could sober up and not smell like vodka when she came home. Those tries weren't easier or softer ways.

For a while, I drank only on days ending with Y. I drank only when my sports teams won. That didn't work. I drank only when my sports teams lost. That didn't work, especially during baseball season when my Pirates lost almost every day. I drank only when it rained or only when it didn't. I drank to warm up on cold days, but I found myself pretending every day was cold, even in the summer. I hid liquor bottles so I could choose to drink whenever I wanted. My wife was better at sniffing out closed bottles than drug-sniffing dogs at the border. Her nose was amazing.

I had to follow the "harder, tougher way" in the *Big Book*. *"Remember that we deal with alcohol—cunning, baffling, powerful. Without help it is too much for us. But there is one who has all power— that one is God. May you find Him now."* God's help *did* work for me. That and nothing else. There is no easier, softer way. Thank you, God, for turning my life around.

Sober day 766
Faith can move mountains but can't put out fires

"Faith without works is dead."

Luke was awakened from a deep sleep by his son.
"Dad, I smell smoke!"
"It must be a bad dream. I don't smell anything. Go back to bed."
The son couldn't go back to bed because flames and smoke filled the hall.
"Dad! Wake up! The house is on fire!" he called back over his shoulder as he ran for the door.
Luke, now wide awake, could smell the smoke but stayed in bed and prayed, "God, you know I have faith in you. I love you and you love me. Nothing can happen without your will as long as my faith is strong. I have great hope and believe in you." Luke coughed, gagged, and eventually was consumed by flames. His son made it outside and survived. Luke prayed, all right. Give him credit for that. But he failed to take action. Prayer alone isn't enough. We have to follow our prayers with appropriate steps, like hightailing it out the door!
Moral of the story: Faith without works is dead. Refer back to sober day 763.

Sober day 769
I'll take a new look at my old brain

I learned online today about existential therapy. I don't know that it's anything new, but it is a new term to add to my psycho-therapeutic vocabulary. Existential therapy can be described as an emphasis on free will and self-determination, centering on the individual instead of on the symptom. The approach emphasizes one's capacity to make rational decisions. It stresses that

- all people have the capacity for self-awareness;
- each person has a unique identity that can be known only through relationships with others;
- people must continually recreate themselves because life's meaning constantly changes; and
- anxiety is a fact of life.

Existential therapy is useful in dealing with psychological problems like substance abuse. The approach deals with people's ability to make choices about how to live, alleviating gunk such as anxiety, apathy, alienation, shame, addiction, despair, depression, guilt, anger, rage, resentment, embitterment, purposelessness, psychosis, and violence. That pretty well describes current and past lives of everyone at any AA meeting. Life-enhancing experiences that can replace those shortcomings include relationships, love, caring, commitment, courage, creativity, power, spirituality, individuation, self-actualization, authenticity, acceptance, transcendence, and awe.

This doesn't sound like anything really new to me, but it does collect a bunch of thoughts and lays them out in a helpful, head-scratching pattern. I'm going to meditate on both my inner-life shortcomings and my life-enhancing experiences listed. Then I'll decide what priorities I need to focus on, replacing the bad stuff with the good.

Sober day 772
Socrates and I realize we know nothing

I drank to avoid my sadness and the too-rapid changes in my life. It felt good. I laughed at what used to make me cry. Drinking was fun, and I enjoyed fun. If it gave me pleasure, I concluded it would give me pleasure again. And again. And again. That's how this addict was created. I enjoyed drinking, and I never wanted to stop. To stop meant discomfort and the return of the sadness I drank to avoid. I needed more and more alcohol to get that same enjoyment. Eventually, no amount brought enjoyment; just sadness all over again.

Ultimately, I found God. It was he who removed my sadness. I rediscovered myself, but this was a new self. Socrates said it well: "I don't know why I did it, I don't know why I enjoyed it, and I don't know why I'll do it again."

Now I *won't* do it again. Socrates also said, "The more I know, the more I realize I know nothing." I wish I had been wiser before alcohol took over. In sobriety, I realize I know nothing. The wiser I get, the less I know.

Sober day 774
Is your glass hope-full or hope-empty?

Step 3: "*Made a decision to turn our will and our lives over to the care of God as we understood Him.*" If there is a God, why would he allow me to drink uncontrollably? When I asked for help to stop, why was there no answer? Why did he watch my life deteriorate into self-destruction? Where was God's love? Where was the joy and peace and serenity I supposedly had been promised? I felt hopeless.

A flip response to my rhetorical questions might be, "Don't give up hope." Yeah, but I once-upon-a-time had hope. Disappointments and time drained it all out of me. Then you can say to me, "Hope is only a word, if you take no action to see AA's promises come true. Don't give up. Don't ever give up. You can't turn away from God who should be our #1 source of hope."

If such frustration is yours, read the *Big Book* from the bottom of page 37 to page 43. I can't do those pages justice by summarizing them here, so read them if you have your doubts about a higher power. Nevertheless, I'll try to provide the *Reader's Digest* version and quote part of the passage here:

> *One of these men, staff member of a world-renowned hospital, recently made this statement to some of us: 'What you say about the general hopelessness of the average alcoholic's plight is, in my opinion, correct. As to two of you men, whose stories I have heard, there is no doubt in my mind that you were 100% hopeless, apart from divine help. Had you offered yourselves as patients at this hospital, I would not have taken you, if I had been able to avoid it. People like you are too heartbreaking. Though not a religious person, I have profound respect for the spiritual approach in cases as yours. For most cases, there is virtually no other solution...* (emphasis added)

"(The alcoholic's) defense must come from a higher power."

Sober day 775
Some are trolls and some aren't

This post today is for Karen. If your name isn't Karen, please read it anyway. I found the following in *Everybody Always* by Bob Goff:

> Trolls aren't bad people; they're just people I don't really understand... There are plenty of people I don't understand. I suppose some are trolls and some aren't. God doesn't see people the way I do, though. The ones I see as problems, God sees as sons and daughters, made in

His image. The ones I see as difficult, He sees as delightfully different. The fact is, what skews my view of people who are sometimes hard to be around is that God is working on different things in their lives than He is working on in mine.

Sober day 777
God doesn't always hold up my bike while I am pedaling

If you're as old as I am, you might remember a time back in the hippie days when the country was fighting a winless war and our leaders were being assassinated and peace rallies turned into riots. We heard the cry many times from many places: *God is dead!* It seemed as though the world was out of control. The captain of the ship had stepped away from the wheel, and we were sinking. There were no lifeboats, just sandbags. I was a kid then. I thought that's the way our existence would be forever. I knew no other social environment. *Maybe*, I wondered, *God really is dead.*

I know better now. Sometimes God *does* step away from the wheel. That's like the way my dad taught me to ride a bike: by holding me up, and then, without a word, letting me pedal on my own while staying a safe distance behind to catch me.

The following is from a book, *Coming Clean*, by Seth Haines. The passage is a little long for this blog, which I try to keep brief, but I find every word worth quoting, and it states:

> Perhaps you know the feeling of fraudulent faith, of adult disbelief? Perhaps it is rooted in your childhood too?
>
> The son who was molested; the daughter who lost her daddy when she was just a girl; the wife whose husband is a disengaged, overachieving, road warrior of a salesman; the husband whose wife has been in an affair for all these years. There are some who have been used and discarded by the church, others who do

116

not believe their worth, their beauty, that they are loved—much less liked—by God. There are those who have been beaten, those who are poor, those who are ever and always on the lesser side of advantage.

Anyone who's been one of these, who's felt the sting of unanswered prayer, shares the same searing question.

Where did our God go?

The bottle is not the thing. The addiction is not the thing. The pain is the thing. So, dear God, let's begin the process of removing the thorns of unbelief. Let's begin the process of dismantling every coping mechanism, of setting them out in the rain to rust.

Our God is still here. He didn't go anywhere, and he certainly didn't die. I found him. He is in me. If he isn't in you, look a little harder. He's there somewhere. I promise. Keep looking.

Sober day 780
Drinking and driving, drinking and dying

I have an AA friend who is a murderer. I'll call him Fred. He isn't afraid to talk about what he did. It's probably good therapy. I'm going to tell an abbreviated version of his story here that's meant to be a disincentive to drive drunk and, for that matter, to drink at all. Period.

Fred woke up one day in a hospital. He had been in a coma and couldn't remember anything. He was told he had been in a serious car accident, but he could remember nothing about it. Then they told him a person in the other car died.

When Fred was discharged from the hospital, he was taken straight to jail and then convicted. He served eleven years in prison. Worse than that, he took a life and permanently changed the lives of the victim's family and friends. He didn't say if the deceased was man or woman, young or old, a parent, or a dependable worker someplace. It was a snuffed-out life caused by another's drinking.

I feel sorry for Fred. He has to carry that guilt with him the rest of his life. I know God forgives him. If only he can forgive himself.

Sober day 781
I'm forever weaving and emerging from cocoons

The older I get, the less I like change, but the more I understand it. What I mean is I mourn the loss of the familiar. I was sorry to watch my childhood home turned into an insurance office. I loved the years I lived in Boise, but I'm disappointed it is so much bigger and different than when I moved there in 1979. My children have changed. I miss their little selves and their little voices; one moved to Colorado, the other turned forty this year. I miss my aunts and uncles. Only one ninety-year-old aunt remains. But in my wise old age, I see the inevitability of change. I've seen two new generations born as we baby boomers watch time tick away faster and faster. The pine and maple seedlings we planted in our yard are now a mature old-growth forest. I remember dial phones changing to push-button, then to cell, now in some cases to watches. The redheaded kid who played with my sisters now is a Pennsylvania legislator.

I am happy to witness my life changing. I'm sorry my muscles have gone stiff on me, but emotionally, mentally, and spiritually, I like the new and improved me. I changed from a child to a husband, to a father, to a retiree, then to a drunk. Then God led me from alcoholism and gave me this new life.

Is there something about you that needs to be changed? Any character defects that need sanded until, gradually, they become dust? One of my recent readings is *The Endless Practice* by Mark Nepo. The author is a confessed poet, and I find his metaphors of metaphors hard to understand. I do understand this excerpt, which describes what I've been trying to communicate to you today. It's the needed change in me as I grow from drunk to recovering alcoholic, and it states:

> Short of being killed, we always emerge
> from difficulty in a stronger if rearranged form...
> By our very nature, each of us is challenged to
> grow out of one self into another. I am not the
> same person I was ten years ago, nor was that
> self the same as the one I inhabited twenty years
> ago—though I am the same spirit. We blossom
> and outgrow selves the way butterflies emerge
> from cocoons.

Sober day 782
Drinking was my "mask of perceived normalcy"

Most of what I read these days is an effort to learn more about myself, about others, and about my higher power I call God. In *Sacred Rest*, Dr. Saundra Dalton-Smith tells about a patient she once treated. The woman had cut her wrists.

> Large brown eyes were not looking *at* me;
> they were looking *into* me... "Do you sometimes
> feel invisible too?" I had never cut my wrist, but
> I was the same as her. I too was medicating my
> loneliness. Not through cuts and self-mutilation,
> but through my own vices. While she resorted to
> a blade, my weapon of choice left little evidence
> of a problem. While she sought relief in watching
> the blood running down her arms, I sought relief
> in hiding behind a mask of perceived normalcy.

Those who cut their wrists are seeking to end their numbness. Some do it for attention. I chose to hide loneliness and sadness by drinking them away, rather than slicing them away. The blood running down my arms was only a metaphor of the damage I was doing to my internal organs.

A suicidal woman and I weren't so different when I was trying to drink away my pain. Her scars remain to remind her of her illness.

My scars aren't quite so visible, but they are there: trips to the hospital, falls downstairs, car accidents I can't remember, the distrust from my family, the lost part-time jobs after retirement, the blackouts, the embarrassments. God chose me to put away my suicidal knife and use my past to enhance others' futures. Without my sickness, I couldn't appreciate my wellness. I crossed a minefield to get here. I thank God for leading me safely across it.

Sober day 783
Love is a gift to be given and received

I love. Not always, but I love: my wife, my kids, my extended family. Those are unconditional loves, and I hope and believe they are two-way streets. I used to think I loved my neighbor as myself. But after self-reflection following my return to sobriety, I'm not sure I was, in reality, traveling that road. I see now that I was so in love with myself that it was hard to love my neighbor as much.

Now that I have turned my life around and allowed God to turn my head around, I can see that I loved, only if I felt loved. I gave lip service to love, and it felt genuine. But I didn't know what I didn't know. My love wasn't really all that genuine. Now my love is about God. God loves me, and his will is that I share his love with others, *all* others. It has to be genuine.

Surprisingly, I find that easy to do. I learned I don't have to love people for what they do but for who they are. I love them because they were created by God, just as I was, and that kind of love now comes naturally to me. Just as much as I love, I crave to be loved. When I feel God's love come to me through others, it's a feeling I never used to have. It's a high far better than alcohol ever was. I am reading *Defiant Joy* by Stasi Eldredge (see the author's video). She writes:

> We are honed both in our needing and
> in our being needed. Whether we are the ones
> experiencing whiplash or the ones walking beside
> those dealing with the aftereffects, there is joy

and growth to be found in the giving and receiving of loving support.

Sober day 784
Seek the beliefs and groups that work for you

I was baptized and raised in a Presbyterian church and continued to attend church when I moved away to Idaho and Washington. I don't go anymore, yet I find the similarities between church and AA to be curious. Going to church and going to AA brings people with similar beliefs together with mostly the same goal in mind: to serve and to help others and to find God. There's a fellowship in both, even though attendees come from differing backgrounds (when I was growing up, our congregation was professional and White, and that includes the students who walked to church from nearby Geneva College. My perception is that churches, like society, have become more diverse as AA is these days. Depending on where you live, you probably can give me a good counter argument to that point).

The big difference I see is that AA doesn't tell you what you have to believe in. Churches insist the Bible is the Word of God, despite many contradictory interpretations of scripture. Believe as they tell you or your next stop is hell. AA says believe in whatever works for you. I like that. I have formed solid beliefs about our spiritual selves, but I keep exploring and remain open to other ideas I may not have thought of yet.

I quoted, two days ago, from Dr. Saundra Dalton-Smith's book, *Sacred Rest*. Here is another snippet I find apropos:

> You can even encounter moments of social rest in brief social interactions where you feel an unusual connection to another because of a shared experience. This is the rest found for many in social groups like Celebrate Recovery (or AA). These groups become a safe place for grace to flow and for the healing benefits of social rest to be manifested. There is *freedom, peace, joy, hope, love, and mercy available* when we find solace in

another. *These gifts change us and make us better people to be around.*

Emphasis added is my own. Seek groups you think "get you." That includes AA, churches, and innumerable organizations.

Sober day 785
Drinking to become uncomfortably numb

I heard this Pink Floyd song during my bleak college days. I wished it were true, but it didn't apply to me. Not then. Not until I was about fifty-five or so. That's when I made it, I thought: I had become comfortably numb. I drank beyond being comfortably numb. I blacked out. I lost control. I was blessed through my first fifty-five years. Then, one by one, the things in my life I cherished, that had made me feel blessed, eroded until I was left with depression and anxiety and alcohol.

> When I was a child I caught a fleeting glimpse
> Out of the corner of my eye.
> I turned to look, but it was gone.
> I cannot put my finger on it now.
> The child is grown;
> The dream is gone.
> I have become comfortably numb.

Thanks to God for giving me my feeling back.

Sober day 786
How God changed my dreams into a better life

Brandy has an unfortunate name for an alcoholic, but she is fortunate that she hasn't had a drink for eight years. She tearfully told us at an AA meeting that she was accepting a job promotion that requires her to move to the Research Triangle Park in North Carolina. Brandy had become sober with the help of several at that meeting, and she was going to miss their love and support. She read a passage from some book about change and its inevitability in life, but I couldn't understand her weeping voice. She asked for some thoughts about change in our lives. Several offered her some encouragement. I did too. The room was packed. It was a meeting I rarely attended, and I knew only a few people there. I told them about Boise. When I was in college, I spent a summer in Idaho, and I loved it. I returned to school in Pittsburgh with a dream of moving to Idaho someday.

Five years later, I was working in my hometown doing public relations at a large steel mill. I was married and just beginning life as an adult—a sober adult, I add here as an aside. By some miracle (clearly God's miracle), I landed a job in Boise. Before long, we had a baby girl there, and three years later, a second. We spent weekends in the summer, camping and hiking in the mountains, never hesitating to take our little girls on the trails. Many people in Idaho shared our love of the outdoors, and we supported the Idaho Conservation League. We attended church every Sunday when we were in town. My wife taught Sunday school, we attended weekly in-home Bible study, and I eventually was selected to the church's session, its governing board.

This is way more detail than I gave at AA, but I want to set the stage here for the point I am about to make. I didn't consider myself ultrareligious or overly spiritual, but I gave thanks for the wonderful life I was living. This was God's will, and it was clear to me he had brought me to Idaho to do that will. I was going to live there forever.

But I got laid off from my job. I couldn't find another PR job in Boise and I had a young family to support. Another layoff victim was working in eastern Washington, and through him, I landed a job in Richland. We left Boise in a snowstorm, and I could hardly see the road through my tears. I got a flat tire on top of a mountain pass and had to change the tire in the snowy, cold darkness. Why, I wondered, did God betray me? It was he who had led me to Idaho that summer and to Boise to grow in my faith and my career and to begin a family. Moving to Washington meant major life changes I dreaded. But wait. I met some wonderful people in Richland and made friends I still keep in touch with. I learned a lot in my new job and explored parts of the Pacific Northwest I never would have seen. We no longer lived at the base of the mountains, but we still lived close enough we could continue to camp and hike. God was still with me.

My wife and I wanted to move closer to family in Pennsylvania. I heard about a job in Louisville, Kentucky, from three different sources. I didn't want to live there but felt as if fate was leading me there. After all, it was driving distance away from our extended family. I got the job, and it was the best job I ever had and the best company I ever worked for. My daughters grew up, earned degrees from the University of Louisville, and met husbands-to-be. My wife didn't work until we had lived in Louisville for a few years. Her volunteer work at the zoo led her to a full-time job and a career there. We were better financially than we had ever been.

Clearly, God led us to Louisville, just as he had led us to Idaho and Washington. I would have missed out on countless benefits of life if I had remained in Boise all these years. Yes, that was my dream. But along came change, unwanted change. All that change was directed by God so that we could fulfill his will for our lives; that is, his will for my wife, both daughters, and me. When change comes along in your life, I suggest you embrace it, pray on it, and see that it doesn't prey on you.

Sober day 787
Getting help in Louisville

Danny, my sponsor, met a woman from Richmond, Virginia. He told her he has met several people in recovery from Richmond. She said the reason for that is in Richmond, it's well-known that Louisville is a good place for recovery. "We get high in Richmond, then come to Louisville to get well." I'm glad Louisville has such a reputation.

Sober day 792
Warning: Alcohol may be dangerous to your health

I took some over-the-counter pain pills because my arthritic knee hurts like crazy today. I searched and searched on the bottle for directions on how many to take and how often. It took me a while because the list of warnings about side effects was so long and the print size was about two point, I think. Drug makers are spending a fortune on TV ads, touting the healing power of this medication and that one, telling us to get some from our doctors. There must be a lot of profit in the medications they are pushing. Along with the miracles any given drug delivers is a long list of warnings.

Don't take it if you're allergic to it (how dumb are we?). Don't take it if you're pregnant or might be. Don't take it if you are diabetic. Don't take it if you ever had a heart attack. Don't take it if you have trouble breathing, if your father has ADD, if you ever had hiccups, or if you were born on a Monday in June. I guess all that is to keep the company out of legal trouble.

What I wonder is why alcoholic beverage bottles don't list all the side effects that come from drinking. They tell you to drink responsibly. What the heck does that mean? I drank responsibly but got pulled over for a DUI the following day. I drank responsibly but somehow ended up at the bottom of the steps with a cut on my forehead. Maybe I simply didn't read the two-point type on the bottle.

Sober day 795
Do more than nip it on the bud

I'm battling dandelions in my lawn. The neighbors don't seem to care, but I accept killing those yellow demons as my mission, now that I am retired and have the time to do it. They are nearly impossible to get rid of. I wrap my hand around the leaves and stem and pull with all my might, but two days later, the dandelion is back, and I can swear it's laughing at me. The only way to get rid of them is to dig them up by the roots or else spray them with poison to kill the roots.

Likewise, to stop drinking, we need to pull alcoholism out by its roots. What does that mean? To overcome our addiction requires more than AA, more than counseling, more than in-patient treatment, more than group therapy. If you're like me, it takes all of the above and maybe more. Kill the roots. Do it now before its seeds are spread by the wind.

Sober day 796
He knocked, but no one answered

I started going to AA meetings again as we ease out of coronavirus restrictions. At this morning's meeting, Darrell lamented his past. "I hated to look in the mirror. It looked like the lights were on, but nobody was home."

Sober day 797
You can't get sober just by thinking about it: take action!

I like Eddie a lot. When he speaks at AA, I know I better be listening. I believe his words come inspired by God because he comes across as being so thoughtful and wise. Eddie is the kind of guy that finding sobriety has taught me to appreciate. There was a time, many years ago, when I would have turned him off. He is covered in tattoos, his hair is unkempt, he rides a loud motorcycle, and he dresses as if he just raided a Goodwill store. I'm glad I have learned to not be so judgmental as I used to be. Oh, I was horrible at that. If someone didn't look like me, act like me, talk like me, or like the same movies I liked, he wasn't worth getting to know.

All that is my introduction to the latest Eddie-ism at AA. He said, "Carrying the message doesn't make me important, but it makes me useful. Simply coming to these meetings won't make you or me sober, but taking action will. Same way, thinking about taking a drink won't make me take one, but action will. Opening the bottle and lifting it to my lips is what will make me drink. Speaking up at meetings and one-on-one with other people is what will keep me sober, care about others. It takes FAITH to stop drinking: *Finally Allowing It to Happen*."

I have come to love all the Eddies in my life.

Sober day 799
God is the doer, not me

 What I write in these passages might pass for a daily reflection. AA also publishes a Daily Reflection, uppercase D and uppercase R. Today's reflection is about humility, a good topic for me. I like this part: "God can only do for me what He can do through me." Humility comes from knowing that God is the doer, not me. The good stuff I do isn't something to brag about because it is God working through me. At least, that's what I pray for daily. "God, your will, not mine, be done."

The Daily Reflection continues: "I am an instrument and any work I seem to be doing is being done by God through me."

I don't know what kind of an instrument I may be, but when I let God, he makes me into an entire orchestra. My friend Eddie had this to say, "True humility is what you do when no one is watching."

Sober day 805
Day by day, sometimes hour by hour, the struggle continues

It's a known fact there is no cure for alcoholism. I long for the days at Kentucky Derby time here in Louisville when I could sip on mint juleps. I miss working in the yard and then sitting on the deck with a couple of cold beers. Those days are over. I fear that if I tried to repeat those relaxing respites that I wouldn't be able to stop until I was blacked out and/or passed out. That's how drinking was for me after years of being able to control it. Page 85 of AA's *Big Book* reminds us of our drinking handicap. "*We are not cured of alcoholism. What we really have is a daily reprieve contingent on the maintenance of our spiritual condition. Every day is a day when we must carry the vision of God's will into all of our activities.*"

Sober day 810
What is my addiction really about?

Danny admitted he used to be a workaholic. I don't believe I ever was one. When part of my job involved after-school activities for at-risk kids, then I was addicted to helping those kids grow up clean and healthy. Working for the big man—no, that wasn't me. I always put in a fair day's work for a fair wage, but at quittin' time, I was in the parking lot.

What about Danny? "Work caused my first marriage to end. Money and work were so important to me. Being addicted to work can be as damaging to your life as being alcoholic."

Shauna Niequist, in the foreword to *Coming Clean*, agrees and says:

> This is a book about alcohol; you can practically smell the gin coming off the pages, the lime, hear the ice clinking, the crack of the new bottle opening. But it's not a book about alcohol. It's about whatever thing you use to cover over the pain—sex, food, shopping, perfectionism, cleaning, drugs—whatever you hold out like an armor to protect yourself instead of allowing yourself and your broken heart to be fully seen and fully tended to by God.

Right, and add work to that list.

Sober day 811
It's all what you're looking for

> On the worst day of your life, something good is happening. You just have to look for it. (Jim at AA)

Sober day 815
What's a relapse?

I should know what is meant by relapse. For a time, Relapse was my middle name. I quit drinking often. Usually, when my wife found the bottle I had so cleverly hidden, I quit drinking. When I woke up at the bottom of the steps with my head bleeding, I quit drinking. When I came to in the emergency room and learned my car had rear-ended another, I quit drinking. When I finished a twenty-eight-day in-patient sobriety program, I quit drinking. I repeat: I quit drinking often. It lasted a month rarely, a week often, a day too many times. I relapsed over and over. I re-relapsed.

Maybe this is playing a simple semantics game, but some differentiate between a relapse and a slip. That way, they can continue counting the days, months, and years of sobriety by claiming, "I didn't relapse. It was only a slip."

Most addiction professionals distinguish between slips and relapses by looking at the addict's intention. A slip is a single unplanned use of alcohol or drugs. Relapse happens when a recovery plan is completely abandoned.

Suppose you are trying on a diet. In a moment of weakness, perhaps at a birthday party with your friends, you eat a piece of chocolate cake. It is a spontaneous decision and confined to that one time. You immediately get back on your diet. This is considered a slip. On the other hand, if you then go get a candy bar at the gas station, buy a tub of ice cream at your next shopping trip, and you completely give up your diet, then that is relapse. Clearly a slip can easily turn into relapse, but it does not guarantee it.

Mark, at one of our AA meetings, told about a relapse that wasn't a relapse and maybe not even a slip. He was someplace and ate a piece of candy. It was a bourbon ball, and it was a mistake. "I discretely spit it into the trash. Was that a relapse?" He answered his own question. "No. I ate it accidentally, and I didn't eat another. When I drank, I sought the first drink. It was no accident. Neither was the second, the third, or the fourth."

Like Mark's, my drinks were no accident. I don't know of a time when I imbibed accidentally. Relapses are unfortunate, but they aren't the end of the world. Relapses and slips are a part of quitting. They happen to the best of us. When they do, confess to your sponsor or to someone close to you. If it's an isolated incident, call it a slip and move on. If your slip is really a relapse, start sobriety over again—one day at a time.

Sober day 816
Mad? Pick up your Big Book and go home

Many of the AA meetings in Louisville are held in churches. Some are held in clubs, like the Pigeon's Roost, the Token III, and E-Z Duzit. Some club members attend AA, others don't. I guess they join for the social outlet. Part of our AA donations go to paying rent at the clubs and churches, but the relationships between clubs and AA in my mind are blurry. Mark told us one time he got mad at the club for some reason and quit going to AA for two months.

"When I decided to return, I walked up the ramp, and Angie was sitting on the porch swing. She asked why she hadn't seen me for a while, and I told her why. She asked me, 'How did that work out for the newcomers?' At first, I was really mad about that comment, but halfway through the meeting, I realized she was right. The meetings aren't about me. They're about others. If I get mad at someone, I shouldn't take it out on the club."

And we shouldn't take it out on others attending AA meetings in search for some wise perspective that will keep them from drinking. I think of that myself when I attend meetings. I go for myself, but mostly, I am there in the event that God might move me to share something or speak to someone after the meeting. I might be able to help an alcoholic. And I might never know if I did help someone. Staying away because I was angry would keep me from doing God's will.

Sober day 817
Should family members be invited to the party?

Here is one more Mark story before we move on. Kat, at an AA meeting, announced she would celebrate her one-year token birthday next week. She couldn't decide whether to invite any of her family members. They haven't been supportive of Kat and her sobriety. They continue to drink and ridicule her for stopping. She asked for suggestions and prayers.

Mark said he faced a similar situation on his first sobriety birthday. His late mother hated alcoholics. She didn't even like to use the word. She *hated* them, even though her son was one of them. Nevertheless, he convinced her to attend his birthday meeting. She fit right in. People welcomed her, praised Mark for his accomplishment, and invited her to visit again anytime. AA was a real revelation to her. "I guess," she told Mark after the meeting, "nice people have problems too."

Sober day 818
Welcome to newcomers

At my home group meeting today at noon we had three newcomers. One was attending her first-ever AA meeting. It's important to make everyone at AA feel welcome, especially newbies. "I like to encourage newcomers to keep coming back until they learn something," Sandy told the group. "And then keep coming back until they teach me something."

We can all learn from anybody. I know people with thirty or more years of sobriety who keep attending AA because they are smart enough to know they don't know everything. There's no cure for alcoholism, so even longtimers can come to see their disease from a little different perspective. A new view might help them if tempted tomorrow. I learn from AA. When I hear something new or clever, I write it in my little red notebook. Those perspectives become new entries in this sobriety diary of mine.

Sober day 819
The old toolbox analogy again

I've compared tricks to stay sober to tools in a toolbox before. Here's another toolbox. I found a card on the counter of an AA meeting place that was titled, simply, "The Toolbox."

1. Don't drink, one day at a time.
2. Ninety meetings in ninety days.
3. Get and call a speaker.
4. Take the Steps 1 through 12.
5. Change playgrounds, playmates, and playthings.
6. Read and study the *Big Book*.
7. Read and study the 12&12.
8. Join a home group.
9. Get involved in service.
10. Find a power greater than yourself.
11. Pray and meditate.
12. Help others.

Sober day 824
Don't let your past define you

Kat, last week, wondered whether to invite her family to her sobriety birthday celebration at AA. See Sober day 817. Her family continued to drink and chided her for making a big deal out of quitting. Well, today was her day, and she clearly decided to invite her family. I guess they accepted her invitation because the room was packed. Extra chairs needed to be brought in. I don't know who was family and who were friends, but they all came out to support Kat. Her sponsor presented her with her 365-day token and invited her to say a few words. She had her comments written on a piece of paper, which she shared with me to share with you, my readers:

> I pray that you have something inside of you that will not break, that will not fade away, that will not fall apart, that will make you able to stand, even if the person you love walks out on you that you cry. But you don't die.
>
> I have smelled the fragrance of his presence, as unworthy as I am. I have this need to tell you that he's amazing. Sometimes, he is the only thing in an unstable world that keeps you from falling absolutely apart. Just goes to show you when you want something bad enough and no longer make excuses, you can do anything you set your mind to and achieve it. Don't ever let your past define who you are today. A forest is not ahead of the seed—it's *in* the seed.

I'm glad Kat's family was there. I hope they were listening. And I hope they understood.

Sober day 825
Slowly, I turned, step-by-step, inch-by-inch

I've written often about AA's Twelve Steps, a key to sobriety when they are followed conscientiously. Before every AA meeting, someone reads the steps as a reminder of their importance. As another reminder of their importance, I'm going to highlight each step, one a week. I will use those seven days in between to give personal consideration to the steps and recommit myself to the process. The Twelve Steps are important to alcoholics, drug addicts, and addicts of every kind. More than that, they are a template of how we should live our lives. God must be in the center of all we do. Further, we come clean of our own shortcomings and seek ways to help others. Only the first step mentions alcohol. The next eleven are a guide for everyone.

I hope you will join me in carefully considering each step and determine how to incorporate them into your life. I plan to add some personal narrative to each. I suggest you get a notebook and do the same. Write what each step means to you. On Step 5, consider sharing your shortcomings with someone else—a friend, a member of the clergy, a counselor, a spouse, and share them with God and yourself as the step states. Make these coming weeks a time to grow. Share this with your significant other, your children, or your best friend. Do the steps together, if you like. Just be sure to explore your inner self.

Sober day 826
Step 1: Admit your life has become unmanageable

"*We admitted we were powerless over alcohol—that our lives had become unmanageable.*" Only by losing can we win. That doesn't make a lot of sense, but it's what we have to do to get our lives back in order. In my case, it took some time because I insisted I could stop drinking whenever I wanted to. It's just that I didn't want to. In-home incarceration and my life was still manageable? What was I thinking? The *Twelve Steps and Twelve Traditions* book of AA, usually referred to as the *Twelve and Twelve*, explains, "We perceive that only through utter defeat are we able to take our first steps toward liberation and strength. Our admissions of personal powerlessness finally turn out to be firm bedrock upon which happy and purposeful lives may be built."

I don't remember for sure what finally led me to accomplish Step 1. Commitment to God certainly figured into my thinking. For quite some time, I told myself that God was okay with my drinking. If drinking weren't part of his will for me, I wouldn't have access to money or transportation to buy booze. See how unmanageable my life had become?

Sober day 833
Looking for Higher Power God

Step 2: "*Came to believe that a power greater than ourselves could restore us to sanity.*" Wait a minute, if I accept Step 2, it must mean I am admitting to being insane. Let's check the scorecard. My wife had a meeting with a divorce attorney. One of my daughters refused to speak to me or be in the same room as me. I was arrested twice for drunk driving. I rear-ended a car and was taken to the emergency room, but I don't remember. I was home, unconscious, and couldn't be revived, so paramedics took me by ambulance to the hospital. Then there was the time...this depresses me. My scorecard indicates I really *was* insane, and I needed God to restore me to sanity. The *Big Book* says, "*Many of us had moral and philosophical convictions galore, but we could not live up to them even though we would have liked to. Neither could we reduce our self-centeredness much by wishing or trying on our own power. We had to have God's help.*"

In my drinking days, I did believe in God. The trouble was that I thought God didn't believe in me. Why else would my life be such a mess? It had to be God's fault. "Valiantly (the alcoholic) tries to fight alcohol, imploring God's help, but the help doesn't come. What then can be the matter?" (*Twelve and Twelve*). I've shared at AA meetings that I believe bringing God into our lives is the most important part of becoming and staying sober. As my boss in Idaho, Linda, used to say, "That's my story, and I'm sticking to it."

Sober day 840
Understanding God's willpower

Step 3: "*Made a decision to turn our will and our lives over to the care of God as we understood Him.*" God is a genie, eager to grant us three wishes. Or no. God is like Santa Claus as long as we are on his good list.

Those analogies sound stupid when we put them on paper. But that's the way some people pray. I did. "God, thy will be done as long as it suits me." I never pray for myself anymore, except to ask

135

that God work his will through me. What I have written here, up to this point, has been, I believe, the will of God. I ask him to help me help others, and if reading these daily passages has helped you, then God's will has been done. "It is when we try to make our will conform with God's that we begin to use it rightly. To all of us, this was a most wonderful revelation. Our whole trouble had been the misuse of willpower. We had tried to bombard our problems with it instead of attempting to bring it into agreement with God's intention for us" (*Twelve and Twelve*).

A note about the "as we understand Him" phrase. Your higher power doesn't have to be the same as mine or your brother or your Aunt Tillie. "Bill's Story" in the *Big Book* carries this advice: "*Why don't you choose your own conception of God.*" All that matters is that we turn over our wills and our lives over to whatever higher power works for us.

Sober day 847
Taking inventory of our character shortcomings

Step 4: "*Made a searching and fearless moral inventory of ourselves.*" I've learned a lot about myself as I worked through the Twelve Steps and listened at AA meetings, counseling sessions, and group therapies. What I don't like about me, I am trying to change. I think that's a never-ending process. That's what makes Step 4 so important. We need to look inward. And next year, do it again. We change. We get better. And maybe we get a little worse in spots. In my case at least, there is still more to work on down the road. And as I trudge that road, even if my shoes fit, they may still give me blisters.

During my month of inpatient therapy at The Brook in Louisville, I was required to write down a list of all my character defects. That's hard to do because we don't see ourselves the same way others see us. Nevertheless, we need to do the best we can to identify our shortcomings. We need to be thorough and honest with ourselves. Dig deep. These personal shortcomings led us to drink, and then more drinking. They have to be exposed to light and fresh air. I like this part of the *Big Book*. I have it highlighted.

"*Selfishness—self-centeredness! That, we think, is the root of our troubles.*" That's me, and I add judgmental to the list of my most serious character defects. "*Driven by a hundred forms of fear, self-delusion, self-seeking, and self-pity, we step on the toes of our fellows and they retaliate... So our troubles, we think, are basically of our own making. They arise out of ourselves and the alcoholic is an extreme example of self-will run riot, though he usually doesn't think so. Many of us had moral and philosophical convictions galore, but we could not live up to them even though we would have liked to.*" Twelve and Twelve advises us to write down our character defects to aid us in clear and honest thinking. "It will be the first *tangible* evidence of our complete willingness to move forward."

Sober day 854
Father, forgive me for I have sinned

Step 5: "*Admitted to God, to ourselves, and to another human being the exact nature of our wrongs.*" Hoo-boy! This is a hard one. I worked Step 5 recovering as an inpatient. My sponsor drove out to The Brook and let me spill my guts to him. I did some pretty horrid and embarrassing things during my lifetime. But some of the confessions I've heard at AA meetings make me sound like cotton candy and lollipops. Still, it was my junk, and I had to unload it all to my sponsor. Writing down my wrongs was an admission to myself. Through prayer, I confessed those same evils to the all-knowing God. So "to God, to ourselves, and to another human being"—a hat trick! That person we confide in might be a sponsor, which worked for me. Other choices might be a clergyman, counselor, therapist, or an AA member who understands what you are seeking to accomplish through Step 5. It can be anyone you can trust to be sworn to secrecy. Some people try to skip over Step 5 or keep some things to themselves. *Twelve Steps and Twelve Traditions* explains that doesn't work:

> If we have swept the searchlight of Step Four back and forth over our careers, and it has revealed in stark relief those experiences we'd

rather not remember, if we have come to know how wrong thinking and action have hurt us and others, then the need to quit living by ourselves with those tormenting ghosts of yesterday gets more urgent than ever. We have to talk to somebody about them.

We have secrets we would rather take to the grave than to another pair of ears. We can't think like that. We need to unburden ourselves. It's important to release the embarrassment and humiliation of our past so that we can move on to a sober life. *Twelve and Twelve* concludes:

> This feeling of being at one with God and man, this emerging from isolation through the open and honest sharing of our terrible burden of guilt, brings us to a resting place where we may prepare ourselves for the following Steps toward a full and meaningful sobriety.

Sober day 861
Get ready, get set, God!

Step 6: "*Were entirely ready to have God remove all these defects of character.*" I thought this step seemed too easy. "Okay, I'm ready, for sure. Now on to Step 7."

Not so fast. Notice the word *entirely*. That means we can't just pay lip service to defect removal. We need to ask our higher power to enable us to move beyond our faults, if we are going to climb the next step. Yeah, but maybe I want to hang on to some of my defects. I confessed to y'all, previously, I looked down my nose at kids who weren't good students or who were unattractive or overweight or couldn't sing well enough to join the chorus. That was wrong of me, but maybe I want to still feel a little bit superior. Just a little bit. And in my career, was my ambition actually greed?

If I talk behind someone's back, that's sharing information, not gossiping. If someone at AA is annoying, that's simply a fact, right? I'm not being judgmental. Wrong, wrong, and wrong. I'm ready, God, for you to remove these feelings. I'll never be perfect. Boy, there's a scoop! But I must continually seek to have God remove my defects of character, including the new ones that have hitchhiked along my adult life. See Step 7. "At the very least," *Twelve and Twelve* tells us, "we shall have to come to grips with some of our worst character defects and take action toward their removal as quickly as we can."

I commit to spend the coming week studying my character defects and making sure I am entirely ready to have God remove them from my curriculum. Only then can I be ready for Step 7.

Sober day 868
Oh Lord, it's hard to be humble

Step 7: "*Humbly asked Him to remove our shortcomings.*" Humbly, it says. "For without some degree of humility, no alcoholic can stay sober at all. Nearly all AA's have found, too, that unless they develop much more of this precious quality than may be required just for sobriety, they still haven't much chance of becoming truly happy," according to the *Twelve and Twelve*.

Our group leader, during my inpatient month of rehab, told about his first experience at AA. He said what stuck with him was that those people were actually laughing. They seemed to be having a good time. He didn't remember "happy." He didn't know how to laugh anymore. His desire for happiness played a big role in his quest for sobriety. As he led our discussions, I noticed his smiles. I remember back then feeling as though, by Step 7, I had come to grips with the fact that I was burdened by my character defects. I was ready to have God remove them (Step 6). And now I pray those defects may actually be wiped clean from my slate.

This Mac Davis song reminds me of what I used to be like, when a lack of humility was a burden to achieving lasting sobriety, and it says:

Oh Lord it's hard to be humble
when you're perfect in every way.
I can't wait to look in the mirror
cause I get better looking each day…

I used to have a girlfriend
but she just couldn't compete
with all of these love-starved women
who keep clamoring at my feet.
Well I prob'ly could find me another
but I guess they're all in awe of me.
Who cares, I never get lonesome
cause I treasure my own company…

I guess you could say I'm a loner,
a cowboy outlaw tough and proud.
I could have lots of friends if I want to
but then I wouldn't stand out from the crowd.
Some folks say that I'm egotistical.
Hell, I don't even know what that means.
I guess it has something to do with the way that I
fill out my skin-tight blue jeans…

Have a listen at:

God, I ask you to remove my shortcomings, and I ask with humility.

Sober day 875
Forgiveness becomes a two-way, four-lane highway

Step 8: "*Made a list of all persons we had harmed and became willing to make amends to them all.*" Steps 8 and 9 leave me quivering in my boots. I have to be honest with you because the Twelve Steps and God make truth-telling a part of my sobriety. So here's the thing: I did make a list of all persons I harmed by my drinking, and I wrote a brief statement of the problems I caused each. I tell myself I am *willing* to make amends, but I never have done so. I'll explain when I write about Step 9.

But first, Step 8. This is about forgiveness. We prepare to come clean with those who are closest to us. We have damaged relationships. In some cases, we probably have strained the friendship and love of those closest to us. Our drinking brought out the worst in us, but maybe it brought out the worst in others too. We need to forgive them as we seek forgiveness *from* them. Seth Haines, in *Coming Clean*, writes:

> I am still holding grudges. I need forgiveness... If the nature of God's forgiveness to me is characterized by my forgiveness to others, I reckon I am a sorry sack... But if falling into addiction is a slippery slope of a process, then forgiveness must be a process too... It requires that I go into the past, that I relive histories again and again until I am able to release all wrongs wrought by the frail humanity of others. I know now what the therapist means when he says I must relive the pain, I must learn to master it.

I have to examine the harm I have done to others. They may have done harm unto me, too, but I have to look past that and forgive them so they might forgive me. "What kinds of 'harm' do people do one another anyway?" asks the *Twelve and Twelve*. "If our tempers are bad, we arouse anger in others. If we lie or cheat, we deprive others not only of their worldly goods, but of their emotional security and peace of mind. We really issue them an invitation to become contemptuous and vengeful."

"Contemptuous and vengeful" describes my wife when I was going through my drinking days. Who could blame her? Well, I could. The first day I started my twenty-eight days of inpatient therapy, I told the director I didn't expect positive results from the experience. "My wife is the one who needs help," I told him. "She is a big part of the reason I drink too much. She needs counseling, if I am ever going to get well." Blaming others is a typical alcoholic tactic. My wife clearly is at the top of my list of people I have harmed.

Sober day 882
Fear of a fall from a "miss-step"

Step 9: "*Made direct amends to such people wherever possible, except when to do so would injure them or others.*" I confessed in Step 8 I was having trouble making amends to people I have harmed. I became "willing" in Step 8, but I feel a little dishonest about that. There were five frogs sitting on the bank. Three were willing to jump into the pond. How many were left? Five. You see, being willing doesn't translate into action.

I don't like reminding the people I have harmed how I harmed them. I fear exposing old wounds. The following passage sure applies to me: "Are there broken places in your life so painful that you fear the breaking will destroy you? Some of the most life-giving people I have met have gone through something that broke them and allowed them to see God use for His glory that which the enemy meant for evil" (*Unstoppable: Running the Race You Were Born to Win* by Christine Caine).

If I make amends, I'm afraid of what it might do to a relationship that appears to have mended already on its own. Digging up old dirt might simply make me dirty all over again. I'm wrong to feel this way, but it's the way I feel. I'm still working on it.

"We will often manufacture plausible excuses for dodging these issues entirely," says the *Twelve and Twelve*. "Or we may just procrastinate, telling ourselves the time is not yet, when in reality we have already passed up many a fine chance to right a serious wrong. Let's not talk prudence while practicing evasion." Maybe, someday, I will get over my hesitation to complete Step 9. I hope so. The *Twelve and Twelve* speaks to me when it says, "Above all, we should try to be absolutely sure that we are not delaying because we are afraid. For the readiness to take the full consequences of our past acts, and to take responsibility for the well-being of others at the same time, is the very spirit of Step 9." I admit I *am* afraid.

Sober day 889
Coming face-to-face with wrong and admitting it

Step 10: "*Continued to take personal inventory and when we were wrong promptly admitted it.*" I don't like to be wrong. When I am, it shows I am imperfect and weak. That all goes back to my childhood when I was so afraid of being made fun of. If I said something wrong, answered a teacher's question wrong, or even laughed wrong, I would feel humiliated. I have since matured to the point of welcoming mistakes because it's mistakes that make us look human. People can relate to us, if they see we have blemishes just like theirs.

Personal inventories come in different shapes and sizes. There's the spot-check inventory, taken any time of the day when we think we might be straying a little bit. Then it's time for us to admit to ourselves and/or to others that we are (ugh!) wrong. Taking inventory at the end of the day is important so that we can evaluate our scorecard and give ourselves credit for jobs well done or acknowledge our goof-ups.

I find, sometimes, it's hard for me to recognize and then control the error of my ways. *Twelve Steps and Twelve Traditions* explains, "When we speak or act hastily or rashly, the ability to be fair-minded and tolerant evaporates on the spot. One unkind tirade or one willful snap judgment can ruin our relation with another person for a whole day, or maybe a whole year. *Nothing pays off like restraint of tongue and pen.* Our first job is to sidestep the traps. When we are tempted by the bait, we should train ourselves to step back and think. For we can neither think nor act to good purpose until the habit of self-restraint has become automatic" (added emphasis is mine).

I am doing a better job of allowing being wrong to roll off my back. After all, other people are wrong sometimes too. None of us is any better or any worse than that guy next to us on the bus. The *Twelve and Twelve* says it well:

> Finally, we begin to see that all people, including ourselves, are to some extent emotionally ill as well as frequently wrong, and then we approach true tolerance and see what real love for our fellows actually means. It will become more and more evident as we go forward that it is pointless to become angry, or to get hurt by people who, like us, are suffering from the pains of growing up.

I can now confess I am sometimes guilty of being wrong.

Sober day 896
On your knees or sit or stand or lie down, it doesn't matter

Step 11: "*Sought through prayer and meditation to improve our conscious contact with God as we understood Him, praying only for knowledge of His will and the power to carry that out.*" My prayers are informal. I don't kneel, bow my head, or close my eyes. I don't end with "Amen." At times, during my day, I carry on a conversation with God. I'm not talking to myself. There really is a God here, always with me, all day, every day. Sometimes I talk out loud, sometimes I whisper, sometimes I keep my prayers in my head. God knows all and hears all. Believing that is an important part of our sobriety. Refer back to Steps 2 and 3.

If it's a scripted prayer you want, look to the Lord's Prayer. Every AA meeting I've ever been to closes with it. Another AA prayer is

known as the Serenity Prayer. I read it on wall hangings before I
ever found my way into AA. You know it: "God, grant me the serenity to accept the things I cannot change, the courage to change the
things I can, and the wisdom to know the difference." Here's another
prayer I have stumbled across somewhere, and again in the *Twelve
and Twelve*. It's known as the Prayer of St. Francis:

> Lord, make me a channel of thy peace—
> that where there is hatred, I may bring love—
> that where there is wrong, I may bring the spirit
> of forgiveness—that where there is discord, I may
> bring harmony—that where there is error, I may
> bring truth—that where there is doubt, I may
> bring faith—that where there is despair, I may
> bring hope—that where there are shadows, I may
> bring light—that where there is sadness, I may
> bring joy. Lord, grant that I may seek rather to
> comfort than to be comforted—to understand,
> than to be understood—to love, than to be loved.
> For it is by self-forgetting that one finds. It is by
> forgiving that one is forgiven. It is by dying that
> one awakens to Eternal Life.

When I was a small child, my mother tucked me in every night
and listened to my prayer: "Now I lay me down to sleep. I pray the
Lord my soul to keep. If I should die before I wake, I pray the Lord
my soul to take. God bless," and then followed a list of extended
family and maybe a few close friends. I don't know when I learned I
was supposed to pray for others and not myself. That came sometime
as my spirituality matured. The *Twelve and Twelve* recognizes such
prayer immaturity:

> Our immediate temptation will be to ask
> for specific solutions to specific problems, and for
> the ability to help other people as we have already
> thought they should be helped. In that case, we

are asking God to do it *our* way. Therefore, we ought to consider each request carefully to see what its real merit is. Even so, when making specific requests, it will be well to add to each one of them this qualification: if it be Thy will (Note to self: Don't use Old Testament King James pronouns like "thy" and "thou" and "thee" in my prayers).

We ask simply that throughout the day God place us in the best understanding of His will that we can have for that day, and that we be given the grace by which we may carry it out.

We have to stop drinking, and we have to never stop praying. I'm not one to quote scripture, but here goes one: "Pray without ceasing. In every thing give thanks: for this is the will of God in Christ Jesus concerning you" (1 Thessalonians 5:17–18 KJV).

Sober day 903
Spread the word: God leads us to sobriety

Step 12: "*Having had a spiritual awakening as the result of these steps, we tried to carry this message to alcoholics, and to practice these principles in all our affairs.*" It's true that I had a spiritual awakening. Without it, recovery would have been impossible. And because I have God in the center of my world, it's only natural that I want to do his will. I don't always, and I don't always know what that will is, but you can be sure I'm wide awake, spiritually speaking. With this step, we turn toward the still-suffering alcoholics. AA members helped me when I was a sobriety pup. They were living Step 12 to my benefit. And now that I am two years, five months, and twenty days sober, it's time that I pay it forward. I seek to help those still struggling and still relapsing, working God's will for my life. God worked through others to help me achieve sobriety. Now he is working through me in the same way.

In *Conversations with God*, by Neale Donald Walsch, the author carries on an imaginary discussion with God. At one point, God tells him, "I will bring you the exact right thoughts, words or feelings, at any given moment, suited precisely to the purpose at hand, using one device or several. You will know these words are from Me because you, of your own accord, have never spoken so clearly." That gives me chills! It describes perfectly the way I feel when I speak out at AA meetings or when I talk to an AA-er before or after a meeting. I sometimes ask myself, "Where did *that* come from?" I got the same feeling at times in writing this blog and book. "Where did *that* come from?"

"Our answer is in still more spiritual development," says the *Twelve and Twelve*. "Only by this means can we improve our chances for really happy and useful living."

Sober day 1,097
The drought continues: three years dry today

Three years is a long time. I was in junior high for three years. I was in high school for three years. I was in college for three years (I got out early on good behavior). I was married three years before my first daughter was born. I lived in Washington for three years.

And now, I have been sober for three years! In all that time, I have rarely been tempted, at least not seriously. My life is so much better! In fact, I think my life is better now than it was before I turned alcoholic because now I appreciate my head being screwed on straight. I can understand addiction, which I couldn't before. God now steers every aspect of my life. God's grace is amazing, just like the hymn says. Nonetheless, there are no assurances about tomorrow. I only have today. I must keep myself sober, just for today. And then do the same tomorrow.

Sober day 1,098
I'm starting with the man in the window

I don't have an ending for this book. After all, sobriety is a process, not a destination. I am sober only for today. Tomorrow, I might have to start all over again. I don't want to do that because I will run out of things to write about. I already fear redundancy. So let me turn to you. My friend Eddie said one day, "I was always looking out the window and not in the mirror."

Well said, and good food for thought. But let me now switch that around and intentionally look out the metaphoric window. Now it's *your* turn for self-reflection. Are you struggling with relapses and "holey" and unholy promises to loved ones? That's where I used to be. I went to AA meetings and group therapy sessions sometimes with a little buzz on because I thought that was the only way I was going to get through them. If this is still you, know that there is a way out. Everyone chooses his or her own road, but the one that seems best to the right destination is the one paved with the 12 Steps. Start with Step 1: *"We admitted we were powerless over alcohol—that our lives had become unmanageable."* Step 1 is the only step that uses the word *alcohol*. The next 11 steps are a pattern for living for everybody.

As for a higher power, Step 2 reads, *"Came to believe that a Power greater than ourselves could restore us to sanity."* Maybe you have successfully gotten yourself through the first two steps. Now is the time to take action. *"Made a decision to turn our will and our lives over to the care of God as we understood Him."* Are you looking into the mirror now? Step 4 states, *"Made a searching and fearless moral inventory of ourselves."*

Maybe you have worked your way beyond all that. Maybe, like me, you have walked the Twelve Steps and are living in some period of sobriety. Then, like me, never lose sight of the new you. Never let the guard who protects you from your next drink to fall asleep on the job. All it takes is one weak moment. Don't let that happen. Have a plan in place so you know what to do if you sense yourself being tempted. Whose phone numbers are at your fingertips that you can call for renewed strength and encouragement? What activities can take your mind off your temptation, like walking or jogging or reading the *Big Book*? Is there a place you can retreat that is really an advance, like the forest or the mountains or a desert? Know right now what you will do in case of a weak moment. Don't wait for that weak moment and then start planning.

I hope something in this book has helped you. Helping others is why God led me to start a blog and to later turn it into a book. Not everything I've written is meant to inspire *you*. But everything I've written is meant to inspire *someone*. If it doesn't, I wasted the paper it was printed on. I don't believe God would have let that happen.

You can do this! I'll never pretend it's easy. Alcohol is a highly addictive toxin that, on the other hand, is a socially acceptable and legal drug. It's fine for some people. But for others of us, we never can let it touch our lips again. It doesn't seem fair. I live in Kentucky, the heart of bourbon country. I would love to sip it the way I see others do. But one man's pleasure is this man's poison. I may not know you, dear reader, but understand that I care.

And understand there is a higher power who cares for you even more. May God bless you and lead you to a life of sobriety.

ABOUT THE AUTHOR

Dan Hicks was born in Beaver Falls, Pennsylvania, to an Ozzie-and-Harriet-type family of the sixties. Church was a key part of the family's life. Dan's love of sports and writing led him into a sports writing job at the Beaver County Times while he was still in high school. His writing ability led to a full scholarship at Point Park College (now University) in Pittsburgh. His career grew into company newsletter editing, corporate communications, business magazine writing, and community relations.

He married Kathy, his childhood sweetheart, and had two daughters. The family lived in Boise, Idaho, Kennewick, Washington, and Louisville, Kentucky. There, Dan served on many community boards and committees, won awards for his work, and was named to the Louisville Communications Hall of Fame. Life was good.

But then his job was eliminated, he couldn't find other full-time work, his marriage became strained, his arthritic knee forced him to give up distance running, and on it went. Everything he cherished seemed to fall apart at once. And so he drank. His successful conquering of alcohol led him to write a blog to share ideas with other suffering alcoholics. It was those daily blog posts that led him to this book and the hope it will help others control their alcoholism.

CPSIA information can be obtained
at www.ICGtesting.com
Printed in the USA
JSHW012107250723
45291JS00005B/163